The Art
of
Organizing Anything

Other books by Rosalie Maggio

The Art
of
Organizing Anything

*Simple Principles for Organizing
Your Home, Your Office,
and Your Life*

Rosalie Maggio

New York   Chicago   San Francisco   Lisbon   London
Madrid   Mexico City   Milan   New Delhi   San Juan
Seoul   Singapore   Sydney   Toronto

1 2 3 4 5 6 7 8 9 0   FGR/FGR   0 1 0 9

ISBN: 978-0-07-160912-8
MHID: 0-07-160912-1

This publication is designed to provide accurate and authoritative information in regard to the subject matter covered. It is sold with the understanding that the publisher is not engaged in rendering legal, accounting, or other professional service. If legal advice or other expert assistance is required, the services of a competent professional person should be sought.

—From a declaration of principles jointly adopted by a committee of the American Bar Association and a committee of publishers.

McGraw-Hill books are available at special quantity discounts to use as premiums and sales promotions, or for use in corporate training programs. To contact a representative please visit the Contact Us pages at www.mhprofessional.com.

Library of Congress Cataloging-in-Publication Data

Maggio, Rosalie.
The art of organizing anything : simple principles for organizing your home, your office, and your life / by Rosalie Maggio.
    p. cm.
  Includes index.
  ISBN 0-07-160912-1 (alk. paper)
  1. Storage in the home. 2. Orderliness. 3. Organization—Psychological aspects. I. Title.

TX309.M34 2009

648'.8—dc22   2008050315

To DAVID
Liz, Katie, Jason,
Matt, Nora, Zoe

Contents

The Art
of
Organizing Anything

Part One

The Secrets of Organization

CHAPTER 1

The Organized Life

There are three kinds of people: those who make things happen, those who watch things happen, and those who wonder what happened.

—Lois Borland Hart (1980)

And three kinds of people will pick up this book.

Some people—and you are the envy of your family and friends—are inherently, comprehensively, and consistently organized. Linda Barnes described an obsessively neat character as someone who "folded her underwear like origami." You may not be at that point, but you could no doubt write a book like this yourself. What you'll find here are some clever tricks to fine-tune your already wonderfully organized life.

Or you may be looking at this book because you are too often the target of unsolicited comments: "How can you *find* anything in here?" "Are you having a garage sale, or is this mess yours?" Family and friends hint that you need to do something about "all this." However, you (a member of a fairly small group) actually manage your life quite nicely in the midst of chaos. If you like the way you live, if the only reason you think you need to get organized is that other people tell you that you do, put this book down. Return to whatever you were doing. When people make rude remarks, do as Phyllis Diller once advised: "If your house is really a mess and a stranger comes to the door, greet him with, 'Who could have done this? We have no enemies.'"

This book was designed for the third type of person. You are frequently frustrated and irritated by your lack of a reliable organizing system in your personal life and your work life. You can rarely find anything on the first go-round. You're habitually running a day late and a dollar short. Worst of all, there's no one to blame but yourself. You've tried to find the culprit—too much work, too small an office, too large a house and, yes, regrettably, the people around you. It wasn't much help when you realized that behind all the confusion and waste of time and money was . . . you.

> *Panic is not an effective long-term organizing strategy.*
> —STARHAWK (1982)

To know whether you need some organizing strategies, ask yourself these questions:

▶ Does the disorder in my life keep me from doing what I want and need to do?

▶ Does the disorder in my life make me feel inadequate and unhappy?

Impairment (being unable to get things done) and distress (feeling angry, frustrated, irritable, or hopeless) are valid reasons for wanting to put some order into your life. When a lack of organization seems to be holding you back and keeping you down, it's time to do something.

Alice Koller wrote, "I've arrived at this outermost edge of my life by my own actions. Where I am is thoroughly unacceptable. Therefore, I must stop doing what I've been doing." If this describes your feelings, you are ready to take action.

What Is an Organized Life?

Only you can answer this. And you need to, because there's no way for you to succeed if you're working toward a fuzzy goal. What would an organized life feel like to you? How will you know when you have achieved it?

> *Too many people, too many demands, too much to do; competent, busy, hurrying people—it just isn't living at all.*
> —ANNE MORROW LINDBERGH (1971)

Set a realistic goal. Maybe you need to rethink only your workplace. Or maybe you do well at the office, but let everything go at home. Perhaps only a couple of areas of your life need attention, and making a few key changes might be enough. You might be happy with being organized 75 percent of the time. Decide at the very beginning what is "enough" organization for you.

Rarely is life "either/or" (either you're a complete mess or you're organized to your back teeth). Aim for somewhere comfortable in the middle.

Some disorder is normal, human, and even desirable. And life is often about things that are half-finished, projects in process, and being in the middle of a job. We need to accept the lack of perfection, the lack of completion, in our daily lives. Finishing some things—not all of them—has got to be enough.

> *Being organized is not an end in itself—it is a vehicle to take you from where you are to where you want to be.*
> —STEPHANIE WINSTON (1994)

Certified professional organizer and president of the National Association of Professional Organizers Standolyn Robertson says, "Being organized is not necessarily the same as being 'neat,' because organization is about function, not appearance." Organizing guru Bonnie McCullough agrees: "To be organized is not synonymous with meticulous. To be organized means you do things for a good reason at the best time and in the easiest way."

In other words, you do whatever works.

The perception that you can't be both tidy and creative is another myth. Most creative people know which skill sets (being organized and logical and tidy, for example) they must shelve when they are creating something. Even so, many highly creative individuals report that they work better in a calm, organized environment. *Messy, tidy, creative*, and *uncreative* are simply adjectives that can be combined in several ways; with human beings, everything is possible.

> *Disorder can play a critical role in giving birth to new, higher forms of order.*
> —MARGARET J. WHEATLEY (1992)

Because there is no one-size-fits-all approach to organizing, this book offers a variety of solutions and suggestions. It's up to you to take the ones that suit you, adapt some others, and forget the rest.

Getting organized is all about you—the way you think, how you work, what makes you feel good or bad, and how you define accomplishment. Some people love colored file folders; others find them messy looking. Some people find that their own clutter makes sense to them; other people find that their clutter is a nightmare. The shelving that solves one person's storage issues would never work for the person next door.

We assume that being "organized" is always a good way to be. And it usually is—but not always. So before you get too deep into bins and baskets and filing systems, ballpark your project to see if the costs and benefits balance each other.

Statistics vary, but it would appear that Americans spend a lot of time hunting for lost items—perhaps an hour and a half to two hours a day, or six weeks a year, or an entire year out of your lifetime. Statistics don't matter as much as how much time you yourself lose looking for misplaced papers or keys or objects. If you spend 30 minutes shopping for a keyrack and hammering it up by the back door, the costs in time and money are a real bargain compared to the time you normally spend looking for your keys. On the other hand, if you lose 20 minutes once a month trying to find a document, it might not be worth bringing in an organizer, investing in a filing system, and attending a workshop to learn how to use it.

Being organized is supposed to make you feel better. If something you're doing along the organizing lines makes you feel worse, stop and rethink the project.

If you've read this far, you're aware of the benefits of being organized (more time, money, and productivity; less stress, frustration, and irritability; fewer errors, missed opportunities, and overdue bills). You may have benefits of your own in mind. Decide what you want more or less of as a result of getting organized.

In some cases, your career could be an issue. Barring exceptional circumstances, most managers would prefer promoting someone with an organized office rather than someone with a messy office. Organization is all about thinking: What is the logical way to group these things or ideas?

Rightly or wrongly, others can't help connecting an ability to organize with an ability to think.

How Much Organizing?

In an intriguing book, *A Perfect Mess*, Eric Abrahamson and David H. Freedman argue that, although "it flies in the face of almost universally accepted wisdom, moderately disorganized people, institutions, and systems frequently turn out to be more efficient, more resilient, more creative, and in general more effective than highly organized ones." They say that "people and organizations are at their best when they've achieved an interesting mix of messiness and order" and that "there is an optimal level of mess for every aspect of every system. That is, in any situation there is a type and level of mess at which effectiveness is maximized, and our assertion is that people and organizations frequently err on the side of over organization."

We can all identify with them when they say, "The unpleasant feeling that each of us should be more organized, better organized, or differently organized seems nearly ubiquitous."

When you think about making changes in your life, recognize the times and places and areas of your life in which a little disorder might not be a bad thing.

In the End...

Consider the possibility that your best efforts might not be enough. This book might not be enough. If you are unhappy—if the emotional fallout from the disorder in your life is overwhelming you—it wouldn't be out of line to see a therapist, at least long enough to understand what's driving your unhappiness.

If you can't function the way you want to—if you hemorrhage time and money and productivity because your "systems" don't work—consider contacting a professional organizer. Get recommendations from friends and business contacts or check out the National Association of Professional Organizers (www.napo.net) and the Professional Organizers in

Canada (www.organizersincanada.com). As of 2008, more than 4,000 professional organizers are at work in the United States and Canada. Also see the National Study Group on Chronic Disorganization (www.nsgcd.org) and individual organizing firms like Vicky Norris's Restoring Order (www.restoringorder.com).

Questions to ask up front:

▶ How much do you charge per hour?

▶ Is there a minimum charge?

▶ Do you charge for travel expenses?

▶ Are there any other charges I should be aware of?

▶ Do you give estimates?

▶ What happens if I need to cancel or change an appointment?

▶ Can you give me some references?

And you are not alone. If you search online, you will find Messies Anonymous (www.messies.org), home of the Organizer Lady; Clutterers Anonymous World Service Organization (www.clutterers-anonymous.org); a Google newsgroup called alt.recovery.clutter; and groups of "clutterbuddies," hoarders, and pack rats.

But, first, check out the 10 simple organizing principles in the next chapter.

CHAPTER 2

The 10 Organizing Principles

*The need for change bulldozed a road down the
center of my mind.*

—MAYA ANGELOU (1970)

I magine the thousands of available organizing systems and tools:
hanging files, colored folders, baskets and bins, labels and tags, marking pens, photo albums, Rolodexes, pencil holders, clothes racks, shoe
racks, pegboard and shelving, curio and linen cabinets, divided drawers,
map chests and hope chests, hooks and hangers, corkboard and eraser
boards, and so on.

Then think of the hundreds of thousands of items that need to be organized: letters, contracts, records, office supplies, meeting minutes, conference brochures, equipment manuals, telephone numbers, addresses, events
tickets, books and magazines, CDs and DVDs and old LP collections,
clippings, family photos, children's drawings, clothing, holiday decorations, yard tools, travel items and luggage, and so on.

Does that make you want to lie down with a cold cloth on your forehead? Me too.

Rather than specify the one best way to organize each aspect of your life,
this chapter provides you with a shortcut to the shortcuts. (Part 3 gives
specific advice, tips, and suggested organizing aids for your office, your
home, your papers, your computer, and your personal life.)

If you familiarize yourself with (and live) the following principles, you can
organize anything—even something that this book, in all its organizational

wisdom, hasn't thought of yet. And the best part is, you can organize it in a way that is natural for you, which means that you are much more likely to get organized and stay organized. It's easier to remember a few commonsense principles than to adopt a "system" that requires a fair amount of effort, time, money, and trying to remember how it works.

Although the principles are numbered, it would be difficult to rank them in the order of their importance in your life. Adopt them as guidelines. If you understand the principles behind each principle, keeping your life a little tidier than it is will soon become second nature to you.

Principle 1: Be Your Own Best Friend

Nobody is making you get organized. You are choosing to read this book. You will choose to adopt 1 or 15 or 60 strategies to organize your life. Everything you do you will be doing for yourself because you want your life to run more smoothly.

Too often we feel that someone is making us get organized, and we get resentful and we rebel. Never mind how we were raised or the bullies on the block or the overbearing teacher we had in sixth grade. The point is, we don't like to be fenced in, and keeping things organized makes us feel a bit oppressed. When you start feeling surly, haul yourself back to the main idea: you're doing this for you.

> Neither situations nor people can be altered by the interference of an outsider. If they are to be altered, that alteration must come from within.
> —PHYLLIS BOTTOME (1943)

Start thinking of yourself as your new best friend. For example, before you leave the office at night, you'll straighten up your desk, shove the papers together in some approximate order, leave your list for the next day in the center of your desk, and push in your chair. When you come in the next morning, you're going to be a happy camper. Whoever was the nice person who did this for you?

When you stop painting for the day and don't take time to put your oil paintbrush in thinner, you return the next day to a ruined brush—maybe your last good paintbrush. A kind friend would've taken a minute to do right by the brush so that you could pick up where you left off and not have to run out to buy another brush.

You don't have to clean up the kitchen before you go to bed at night, but it's going to be you walking into the kitchen the next morning. Maybe you don't mind dried food on plates. Truly, that's all right. But if you like to start the day with a clean kitchen, do yourself a favor and clean up the night before.

Make a habit of taking a few minutes to tidy things whenever you stop working on something. Maria Montessori used to teach her young pupils that the work was not finished until the table was cleared and their chairs were pushed in. Your work isn't finished until you've left things the way you want to find them when you return.

As a corollary, organize to please yourself. Unless you share an office or a closet with someone, you get to do things your way. Because your choice of whether to have open shelves or a closed cabinet or whether to have hanging files or stacked files springs from your own tastes, you are more likely to support them. If you choose colors and designs that are pleasing to your eye, you're more likely to keep their surfaces clean.

It's all about you. Every bit of organizing that you do is going to make your life easier. When you lose a button from your shirt, there's a sewing kit ready to go. When you want to lend a business book to a friend, you know where to put your hands on it. When you need the car, it's fairly clean, there's meter change in the glove compartment, and it even has gas. When you want coffee, you have not only coffee but filters and sugar in the cupboard and milk in the refrigerator. It's much like having your own servant or assistant, someone who keeps your life running smoothly.

The mindset you want is one that looks forward to the next time you return to this spot. And the key to looking forward is looking behind.

Before you leave a room, look behind you. What needs putting away, cleaning up, or jotting down? Will you find the file where it belongs, or will you have to spend half an hour looking for it? Will your desk be cleared for takeoff, or will you despair at the thought of digging in? Will you find enough laser paper to run off 10 copies of the report, or will you have to go get some? Will your tape dispenser be ready to roll, or is it still as empty as you left it?

Before you leave the sales counter, look behind you. Did you leave a briefcase, packages, or an umbrella? Before you leave a meeting, look behind you. Did you leave a jacket, papers, or your purse? Before you leave your car, look behind you. Is there trash to be disposed of, something to be carried into the house, or a forgotten box in the backseat? Before you leave the kitchen, look behind you. Did you clear off, put away, stack in the dishwasher, and otherwise leave no tracks?

What it comes down to is that being organized is about being nice to yourself—doing what is needed so that when you return to a spot an hour, a week, or a month later, you'll find things all ready to go—with the emphasis on being able to find things.

You'll have many opportunities to be grateful for your new best friend.

Principle 2: Reduce Every Task to Its Smallest Parts

After you set a goal ("organize my office"), break down the job into the smallest possible steps ("clean out my middle drawer," "organize my office supplies shelf," "clear off the top of my desk," "gather my files on the Fresher project and collapse them into one file, weeding out duplicate and unnecessary material").

To organize your kitchen, do it drawer by drawer and cupboard by cupboard. If you're landscaping, divide the area into sections (northwest side of the house, northeast side of the house) or into type of work (planting bulbs, sowing grass, weeding, installing a fence).

Never start a job without dividing it into logical smaller tasks. And always finish one task before going on to the next, even if they seem related.

If you're working on a project with a deadline, after dividing the job into parts, work backward from the due date to assign an intermediate deadline for each part of the project.

Principle 3: Like Belongs with Like

If you remember only one principle, choose this one. Failing to understand that things "belong" with others of their kind is the most basic problem for the disorganized. It should be impossible for someone to toss a rubberband into the paperclips box. But it's not.

If you already have a sense that all reams of paper go on the same shelf, that all your pens and pencils go in one holder, and that all the potholders stay in the same drawer, you are ahead of the game.

Children are taught to distinguish which one of a group of items "doesn't belong." IQ tests ask which object is not like the others. Like things belong together. If you have to, imagine that the unanswered letters scattered on your desktop, file cabinet, worktable, and shelves are crying for their brothers and sisters. They *want* to be together. Help them.

Hold up any object and say, "Where does this belong? Where are other things like it?" If nothing occurs to you, put it in your ? pile (see Principle 7) and go on to the next item.

Whatever you're organizing, begin by sorting things into piles of similar items. Next, put each group of like items into its own file folder, bin, basket, tray, or drawer, or on its own shelf.

The hard part about being organized is not getting organized, but staying organized. Label items clearly or keep them in see-through containers so that you can (1) find things quickly and (2) put things away correctly.

If you live with others, give them a walking tour of newly organized areas so that they too can find things quickly and put things away correctly. Labels are especially helpful when more than one person is using the items.

Principle 4: Cluster Similar Tasks

In addition to grouping like objects, we need to group activities to save time, money, and energy, and to keep the tops of our heads from blowing off.

Never run an errand without doing all the errands in that part of town. If you have only one errand, put it off (if possible) until you have another two or three things to do nearby. It's rarely efficient to deliver only one file to the second floor, wash just one load of laundry or only half the dirty dishes, order only two items from the office supply store, or go to the post office twice in one day. Sometimes things need to be done this way. In general, however, try to be like the older woman who said that every time she bent over to tie her shoes, she looked around to see what else she could do while she was down there.

► *Group errands.* Never go to the bank without also picking up the dry-cleaning, dropping off your rental movies, unloading a bag of good used clothes at the Salvation Army, and getting gas. Or whatever. If you live a halfway organized life, there should be no need for emergency runs involving one stop. Always combine your errands.

Dedicate a convenient space in your office and by your door at home where you can place items that are going elsewhere: gloves that someone left behind, library books to be taken back, drycleaning to be dropped off, DVDs to lend to a coworker, letters to be mailed, a casserole dish belonging to a neighbor, a roll of quarters for parking meters, or your latest auto insurance card that needs to go in the glove compartment. Each time you leave your office or home, check the pile to see if anything's going your way. Even more convenient, post a comfortably large carryall near the door or even hanging on the doorknob and stash outgoing items in it, ready to go.

After a while, checking the "outgoing" area for anything that can be taken to its destination on this particular trip becomes a habit.

Anything that is leaving your house must be put in that place, and no other. In this way, you can do away with some of the irritation of not being able to find something when you're on your way out.

► *Group appointments.* Schedule your annual medical checkup the same day as one of your six-month dental visits, and maybe add in a visit to the optometrist. Grouping appointments like this means that you can focus on your health, make connections between a dental and a medical problem, for example, and save multiple visits to the same clinic.

► *Group phone calls.* A great time-saver is returning all phone calls at the same time of day—a time of your choosing. You can decide whether an exception truly needs to be made, but you'll benefit enormously by focusing on what you're doing and ignoring phone calls during the rest of the day. When it's time to return calls, you'll tend to be brisk and businesslike because you have six of them to return before you leave the office. If you answer calls duck by duck, the temptation is to linger with each caller.

► *Group e-mails.* Check your e-mail only once or twice a day, and respond briefly. As with phone calls, when you answer one at a time, you spend twice as much time on that e-mail as you would if you knew that you had 15 more to write.

▶ *Group chores.* If you can schedule all your meetings in one afternoon (something that's not always possible, of course), you can put yourself in meeting mode and barrel through all of them, saving the rest of the week for uninterrupted work. If you're washing the windows in a room, carry your equipment to the next room, and the next, and wash all the windows. Another way of looking at it is by area rather than by task. If you're organizing a bedroom closet, do the drawers too—and perhaps the rest of the room while you're at it. If you've asked someone to organize the supply room, have them check with everyone in the department for supplies that should be returned from people's offices to the supply room or vice versa.

▶ *Group events.* As long as you've done all the work for a birthday dinner, invite a neighbor (perhaps someone you've been meaning to see for months) to come and have tea in your spanking clean house that afternoon. When the yard is shipshape for a family reunion Sunday afternoon, invite close friends to come for leftovers that evening. Nobody said this was easy, but once you start grouping things, you think about the superclean house, the napkins you had to buy anyway, and the serving pieces you already retrieved from the top cupboard, and you can stack events.

Principle 5: Start Wide and Then Narrow

Always begin by pulling out and gathering everything that is related to the job at hand. If you need to make some sense of the paperwork on a project, collect all the files, letters, reports, clippings, memos, printed e-mails, records of phone conversations, and faxes that deal with it. This includes copies of material that coworkers may have. Don't even think of starting before you have everything before you. This is starting wide.

As you sort according to topic, stapling some papers together and discarding others, you will narrow everything down to a manageable file.

If you're organizing your jewelry, gather it all together from your several jewelry boxes, the bottoms of purses, coat pockets, items you've lent to others, dresser drawers, the kitchen counter, the bathroom shelf, your children's toybox. Do not start until you have everything in front of you.

It's almost impossible to sort office supplies or winter clothes or canned goods or postage stamps efficiently if you can't see everything you've got.

Principle 6: Sort

Once you have everything laid out and you've put like with like, you begin sorting.

Sorting is the foundation of organizing. Some people have an inborn sense of "this goes with that." If they walk into a kitchen with a used glass, they will put it with the other unwashed dishes. The person born without this faculty has paperclips and pens and loose change and single postage stamps in every drawer in their desk. The first type of person thinks of items as magnets for other things like themselves and automatically groups similar objects. If you're the second type of person, keep practicing (and chant to yourself "like with like" as you sort).

Be prepared with a trash can, a wastebasket, or a garbage bag and with a marking pen and labels or sticky notes. But don't buy bins and boxes and other "organizers" ahead of time because until you've finished sorting, you won't know what you've got and what you'll need.

Each item goes into one of four piles:

▶ You're keeping this (Keep).

▶ This goes in a garbage bag (Toss).

▶ That will be given to someone or set aside to be repaired (Give-Away).

▶ You're not quite sure what to do with this (?).

Depending on what you're doing, you might have a fifth pile, to be stored. If you come across a handful of tree ornaments (whoever could have put them there?), they get set aside to go out to the garage or up to the attic with the rest of the ornaments. You might store all the baby clothes that have been outgrown by this baby but might come in handy for the next one in an airtight plastic bin.

(The Toss pile will include items to be recycled.)

As you decide each object's destination, put it with others of its kind so that you have piles of like objects.

Principle 7: Your ? Pile

What stops most of us in our tracks when we're organizing are the items that we don't know what to do with. Maybe Grandma could use it. No, there's a chip. Maybe I could repair it. Even if I did, I don't think I like it. I wonder if it's good enough to give to Goodwill. Who gave us this thing, anyway?

And there we sit. Some items do not appear to belong with any other items. You can't think of the most logical place to put them. You can't decide among Keep, Toss, and Give-Away.

Fortunately, there is another pile: the ? pile.

As you're making decisions, immediately put anything that you can't quickly categorize in the ? pile. Don't be stopped by these items. They will demoralize you, slow you down, and often stop you altogether.

That pile will grow until you've finished the current job. By then you may have a clear idea of where those items belong or whether some of them should be tossed.

Don't despair if, even after the entire office or bedroom is organized to your liking, you're left with a small ? pile. Just move that pile along to another place—preferably to the next location you've selected for organizing.

If, after you have organized your entire personal life, your entire professional life, and your neighbor's life too, you still have a ? pile, that's okay. Someone who has organized their entire personal life, their entire professional life, and their neighbor's life too is not afraid of a small ? pile.

By now, you have the strength of ten. You fear nothing. You will know exactly where those items go.

Principle 8: Everything Has a Place

You've heard it all your life. Isabella Beeton first said it in her 1861 classic, *The Book of Household Management*: "There should be a place for everything, and everything in its place." We tend to remember "everything in its place" but forget the importance of "a place for everything." If you have no keyrack by the back door, of course you will have keys on the buffet, on the kitchen counter, and under the sofa cushions. If you have not provided for the family's snowboots, they'll be leaning and dripping on the front porch, back porch, the back entryway, and the front entryway, and maybe in the kitchen. If you have magazines and newspapers covering most surfaces in the living room, you obviously don't have a magazine rack or a dedicated spot on a shelf for them.

It's possible that your office has thousands of items (especially if you count paperclips) and that your home has hundreds of thousands of items (especially if you count potato chips). In any given day, you'll be taking out and, one would hope, putting back many of these items. If they don't have a place, (1) how can you find them? and (2) where will you put them when you're finished with them?

When you repeatedly find items lying around, look to see if they have a home. They may not. Organizing authority Bonnie McCullough says, "Very seldom do you save time putting things down in temporary spots." Everything needs its own home.

Theoretically, your office or desk area should be so logically arranged that you could find things with your eyes shut. If you always return the stapler to the same spot, you can find it instantly, and putting it back there should be equally simple.

Most of us are living in less space than we feel is comfortable for us. To get around this, your spaces need to be organized. If you have gone through your office and home and made a decision to Keep, Toss, or Give-Away every item (except for the ? pile), you have bettered your situation enormously.

What might be left is finding homes for the items that didn't fit neatly into existing places. For this, you might need what are euphemistically called organizers (as if they had brains). But you can make good use of bins, boxes, shelves, baskets, trays, containers, and other items to keep like things together. In Part 3 you'll find specific suggestions for organizing solutions to use at work, at home, and at play.

When you are finding a place for everything, make sure the place makes sense to you. House items close to where they are used. House them where they are handy (if you use them often) or out of the way (if you don't use them often). Your system must make sense to you. Don't put something in a cupboard simply because you had a little extra room there. Put it where you will look for it.

Use the four-point plan for putting everything in its place:

▶ Keep (find it a logical place)

▶ Toss (it's broken, unusable, or unrepairable)

▶ Give-Away (someone else can use it)

▶ ? (not sure yet what to do with it)

It may seem counterintuitive to be told to spend time organizing your life when time is exactly what you're short of. But spending one hour setting up a central location for all the paperwork in your house will save you many hours of hunting for a permission slip or a doctor's appointment card or a bill in time to avoid finance charges.

Put like items in as few different places as possible, and be consistent. Don't have key hooks at the front, back, and side doors—you'll never know where your keys are. In your office, all reference files should be in the same file drawer, or in neighboring drawers if you have a lot of them. All envelopes—business, manila, and bubble mailers—should be near each other.

Principle 9: The 15-Minute Rule

The 15-minute rule posits that just about anyone can do just about anything if it's only for 15 minutes. The corollary is that if you can persuade yourself to spend 15 minutes on something, you may reach what Shakespeare called, in a different context, "the sticking point." After 15 minutes, either you will be rolling along so well that you will continue or you will be able to stop, knowing that you've made serious headway and can return to the task without having to bribe or threaten yourself.

No time like the present.
—MARY DELARIVIÈRE MANLEY
(1696)

A related suggestion is that you do your 15 minutes now. Fifteen minutes fits nicely between bigger chores in your day. Some tasks can be completely finished in 15 minutes. Bigger jobs can look smaller after you've worked on one of their elements for 15 minutes.

It's the starting that's hard. Mark Twain is supposed to have said, "The secret of getting ahead is getting started." If getting started looks like a huge, involved, days-long project, you're not likely to want to get started. But if it looks like just 15 minutes, you might be willing to do it. And, once you've talked yourself into 15 minutes, start now. Only some wines and cheeses get better with waiting. Jobs tend to grow fat and menacing with time.

Principle 10: The 80/20 Rule

If you are familiar with the 80/20 rule, which has been around for some time, you are excused from this section. If you aren't, stay. This is useful.

In 1897, Vilfredo Pareto, an Italian economist, observed that 80 percent of income in Italy went to 20 percent of the population. He went on to observe that 80 percent of the wealth in Switzerland was held by 20 percent of the people. In the 1930s and 1940s, business thinker and quality management pioneer Dr. Joseph Juran elaborated on what he called the Pareto Principle, and concluded that our lives consist of the "vital few" (20 percent) and the "trivial many" (80 percent).

Here are some possibilities:

► 20 percent of the defects cause 80 percent of the problems.

► 20 percent of customers produce 80 percent of sales.

► 20 percent of employees take 80 percent of sick leave.

► 20 percent of the people we know are responsible for 80 percent of our interruptions.

► 20 percent of your staff will cause 80 percent of your problems.

► 20 percent of your staff will provide 80 percent of your production.

► 20 percent of your efforts produce 80 percent of your results.

► 20 percent of drivers will cause 80 percent of auto accidents.

► 80 percent of our time is spent with 20 percent of the people we know.

- ▶ 80 percent of telephone calls come from 20 percent of callers.
- ▶ 80 percent of the time we wear 20 percent of our clothes.
- ▶ 80 percent of file usage involves 20 percent of your files.

Although the 80/20 rule is neither exact nor infallible, it provides a handy way to think about how we spend our time. Timothy Ferriss, author of *The 4-Hour Workweek*, actually recommended getting rid of the 80 percent of your customers who take up the majority of your time and focusing on the 20 percent who make up the majority of your profits. That's up to you, of course.

What the 80/20 rule should be saying to you is: Which 20 percent of the items on my To Do list really matter? Where is the 20 percent of my work that is going to pay off big time (80 percent of the payoff)? What 20 percent do I need to focus on? Is this item a low payoff (one of the trivial many) or a high payoff (one of the vital few) item? If I have to let something slide today, let's find one of the "trivial many" to ignore.

By reflecting on, and making a habit of, these 10 organizing principles you will discover that your life is more orderly in small and large ways. You will automatically become a good friend to yourself. When you undertake a large organizing project, you'll find that you're halfway finished before you've begun. In the next chapter, you'll gain control of an outstanding organizing tool, one that underscores and maximizes all 10 principles.

CHAPTER 3

The Single Most Powerful Organizing Tool

*If you keep everything on your mind in your
mind, you could have brain clutter.*

—LAURA STACK (2004)

W hat is the single most powerful organizing tool? If you're expecting something with rechargeable batteries and artificial intelligence, prepare yourself. Your other new best friend is the *list*. The lowly list. Water ("weak as water") carves channels in massive rocks, smooths rough stones, and makes waves big enough to overturn battleships. With a great deal less drama and time than water, the list can revolutionize your life. I promise.

If you are an astonishingly unorganized list maker or you have not yet got the hang of it, stay with us. Even if you think you are not the type who can profit from a list, keep reading because your type doesn't matter. What matters is the type of list you keep.

People who don't keep lists are obliged to keep everything in their heads (or on scattered bits of paper that are never where they need them). The list-less among us resemble a

I have a secret. I make lists. That's how I handle stress. And whether they actually help me accomplish more or not, they make me feel so much better. If I can jot down all the tasks that swirl around in my head, I shift from feeling deluged and stressed to feeling in control and calm. And this is before I even do anything on the list.

—SUZANNE RISS (2007)

computer with heavy-duty indexing programs running in the background, stealing memory and speed. Something's constantly ticking over in the back of their brains—remember to do this, don't forget that. Not only do they sometimes not remember everything, but this low-level buzz also cuts the effectiveness of everything else they're trying to do.

If part of your attention is on the past (something that you forgot to do) or on the future (whatever you're going to do next), you're not giving your best to the job at hand. Lists clear your head of items you don't need to be thinking about.

The alternative to keeping a list is making a special trip to the store for olive oil, overlooking a birthday, sending in your rebate too late, forgetting that this is the week your assistant is on vacation, paying finance charges for a missed due date, or leaving messages for three people asking where the meeting is being held this time.

Some individuals, it's true, can live a successful, happy life without ever making a list. If that's you, good-bye and godspeed (all three of you). The rest of us can find our lives simplified, our stress lowered, and our free time increased by taking a few minutes here and there to tend our list.

List or Lists?

Referring to one list is simpler and sounds less confusing. In addition, talking about "a" list emphasizes that all your notes need to be in one place. However, your list will have various parts to it.

Where to Keep Your List

Where you keep your list depends on what suits you. The requirements are as follows:

- ▶ All notes, all parts of your list, must be in one place.
- ▶ In general, you must be able to access your list from wherever you are.
- ▶ You must keep a backup copy of your list.

The most convenient and effective place to keep your list is on the computer that you use every day. If you move back and forth between a desktop and a laptop, use a flash drive or USB stick to copy your list from one to the other. If you are going to be away from both computers, print out the part of the list that you'll need when you travel or go home for the day or when you run errands or go shopping.

As for how to keep lists on your computer, the very simplest, lowest-tech method is to open a file named "To Do" or "Lists" or whatever title means something to you, and keep linear lists. For the high-tech among us, a plethora of software exists to help you with your list. But take some time to find something that works the way you work, that feels comfortable, and that you actually enjoy calling up.

If you like it and will use it, an eminently portable electronic planner—iPhone, BlackBerry, PDA, or other similar electronic device—might be a great choice for you. However, don't forget to back up your list somewhere else. It's easier to lose one of these than to lose your desktop.

A notebook, daily planner, diary, personal organizer, or journal can contain all your lists. It's a little messier when you cross out items or move them from one day or one list to another, but if this suits you, then buy a notebook that is pleasing to your eyes, along with, perhaps, a special pen that will make keeping up with your life a sensory pleasure.

If all your invaluable lists are in one notebook, however, the fear of losing it may outweigh the comfort it brings you. One woman put a tag in her notebook offering a $50 reward to anyone who returned it. This may work eventually, but in the meantime, you don't know where you're supposed to be in an hour.

Backing up (and keeping current) a handwritten notebook is a little more time-consuming. But for your security of mind, you must do it.

If you live with others, an important adjunct to your list is the communal calendar. Only those events, appointments, and activities that occur during family time or that involve other family members need to be put on this calendar. Get a big one and post it in a central area, preferably near a phone. Attach a pen to it so that the pen doesn't develop legs and take off.

If your whole family is computerized, you can all input items into the common family computer calendar.

Making Your List

► Write down absolutely everything in your life that you need or want to keep track of or to accomplish. *Everything.* And put all the things you write down in one place. *One place.* You will be jotting notes to yourself here and there, but as soon as you can, transfer them to your central list. The most important principle is: *everything in one place.* When you do this, you have the security of knowing that nothing will be forgotten, nothing will go undone.

► Promise yourself that if something gets onto your list, it will get done. Maybe not now, maybe not even soon. But it will get done. In the meantime, you don't have to worry about that item—it will not be forgotten. The corollary is never to put anything on your list that you are not going to do. If you think it would be "nice" to alphabetize your software manuals, but you rarely refer to them, don't assign yourself this job. Don't even put it way down at the bottom of your list. It'll just send off unpleasant vibrations from its place down there, and when you never get around to doing it, you'll lose faith in yourself as an I-do-what's-on-my-list kind of person. The more strongly you believe that the items on your list will be taken care of, the more relaxed you will be, and the more likely you are to do them. Every time you cross something off your list, your confidence in yourself will grow.

Success breeds confidence.
—BERYL MARKHAM (1942)

► Your list won't be much use to you if it's a jumble of items:

Cancel order

Buy eggs

Call Frank

Pool tournament Friday

Return library book

Pick up drycleaning

Finish report

Find replacement tiles

This is a good way to start, of course. You'll be jotting down things as you think of them, and you want to include absolutely everything that's on your mind. But when you add them to your list, they must go into categories.

In addition, this list leaves a lot to the imagination. Which order? Do you have an order number and phone number for it? What's Frank's telephone number? Which Friday and what time and where is the pool tournament? When will the drycleaning be ready? How many replacement tiles? And "finish report" has a whole list of possible questions all by itself. It also sounds like such a huge job that you'll probably want to do anything except that.

When you add an item to your list, include everything that will make it easier for you to accomplish that task: date, time, phone number, address, directions, size.

Types of Lists

The way you categorize the parts of your list is what makes it specifically your list and what makes it easy for you to use. You can organize your list by types of tasks (phone calls, meetings, errands); by days, weeks, months, or years; by deadlines; by short-term and long-term tasks; by things you need to do and things you want to do and things you're still dreaming about. Nobody needs every one of the categories listed here. Choose the ones that will be most useful to you.

▶ *Today.* Whether you call this list Monday or April 3 or To Do, this is your first and most important list. It's what most of us think of when we talk about our list. On this list goes anything that comes due today or that absolutely must be done today. To those necessary items, you can add several items that you would like to get at today and that you actually have some hope of getting at. As you get better at list making, you'll be able to judge just how much you can put onto one day's calendar.

▶ *This Week/This Month.* You may not need this category, but some people like to have a feel for how the week or the month is going to play out. As on the Today list, everything that falls due in the coming week or month is noted here.

▶ *General.* Unless your life is complicated enough to warrant some of the remaining categories, you can pretty much throw everything that isn't dated (see the next point) or happening today or on your shopping list in here.

▶ *Dates.* You can call this Tickler File or Coming Up or Action File or Commitments or anything else that works for you. This is the one place where you keep track of all events, activities, ongoing projects, tasks with assigned dates, and timed reminders to yourself (every six months, "call for DDS appt."; once a week, "back up computer"; four times a year, "estimated taxes due"). For example:

- July 16, 12:00 p.m.: Rotary meeting, Wahkonsa dining room (bring Italian road atlas to lend Fran)
- July 16, 6:30 p.m.: Jeannie's softball game, Expo park
- July 18: Are budget papers ready for Stevens Corp.?
- July 18: Call 818-444-5555 for results of bone density scan
- July 19, 10:00 a.m.: Conference call with Stevens (Bill setting up the call; need budget papers)
- July 20: After 6 p.m., call 661-343-5555 to see if our group has been called for jury duty
- July 21, 8:15 a.m.: Jury duty; 1411 Truxton?
- July 25: Call bank (431-4412) to cash out CD
- July 26: Pick up penicillin at drugstore; call 612-241-5555 first to see if it's ready
- July 28, 11:00 a.m.: Dentist appt., Dr. Mascia, 641-242-5555 (take penicillin four hours before appt.)

▶ *Shopping.* You may have a pad of paper in the kitchen to note items you're getting low on, but regularly transfer those penciled notes to your main shopping list. List the items in categories: groceries, office supplies, hardware, pharmacy, garden center. Then, when you're heading out, you have to print out only the appropriate part of the list. It will save you time if you organize the groceries you need the way your store is laid out. At the least, list together all fruits and vegetables, dairy products, frozen goods, and bakery items.

▶ *Won't Do.* This won't be the first list you draw up, but as you find that there are some things that you aren't good at doing, that you don't value enough to do, or that you just frankly don't want to do, make a list of them.

One of the reasons our lives spiral out of control is the number of unexpected invitations, requests, and demands on our time. If we could chug-chug along on our usual tracks, taking care of work, home, health, family, and friends, we'd keep busy, but we could probably manage. Instead, we're called upon to fundraise, babysit, attend a wedding, go to a conference, substitute for a friend, or take a sick colleague's meeting.

Make a list of your no-no's. Then rehearse several sentences to tell people, "I'm sorry, I can't."

You might be willing to sit on your local museum's board, but you are lousy at fundraising (because you hate it), so you might decide that you will never fundraise for the museum (or for any group). Write it down. Follow it with a sentence like: "I'm sorry, I don't do that." "I'm sorry, I can't help you." "Thanks for asking, but I have to say no."

Don't explain. It's a temptation to elaborate: "Listen, I'm such a poor fundraiser, you wouldn't want me." This simply encourages the other person to assure you that they have a training meeting that'll give you wings.

Keep repeating your sentence: "I'm sorry, I can't help you."

When you are prepared—when you know precisely what makes you miserable and you have a good "no" line—you can handle random requests without guilt or uneasiness.

You may have already said yes to things you regret (you're involved in an unsatisfactory carpool or you've been drafted to take meeting minutes). This is a good time to examine your life and see where you're losing vital energy and time.

Don't feel guilty because you're saying no to some essentially positive request (fundraising for a neighborhood garden). If it were evil, saying no wouldn't be a problem. Our busyness stems from our having a surplus of worthy activities available to us. When in doubt, say to yourself, "If I were two people, one of them would do this. But, sigh, I am only one person."

Sometimes we mistakenly feel that we "owe" people something. A good guideline here is that if you are crouched in your closet gibbering from a surfeit of life, you will be no good to anyone. You owe it to yourself to be sane. A good guideline is that the things in life that we are supposed to do are not heavy. It's those tasks that we take on because we "ought" to that make us miserable. When we are doing the things that we have a gift for or when we want to help out, the task is light. Anything that feels too heavy is probably not a good choice. Admittedly, there are times when we do hard things for others because they must be done. You know the difference.

The Won't Do list stiffens your backbone. When you have thought through the kinds of things you are unwilling to do (serve on committees, have a dog, take long car trips, babysit for neighbors, do tax returns for friends), you are far more likely not to impetuously take in a stray dog or say yes to doing the tax returns. There's no point in agonizing every time a decision presents itself—you know from experience that you always regret taking on this particular chore. Say no.

▶ *Goals.* Some people know that they're going to travel to the Himalayas, buy a home, or raise goats. They don't need to write these things down. But people who actually write down their work goals or their personal goals seem to accomplish them more effectively than those who don't. However, a goal (buy a house) isn't something you can really work with. That goal has to be broken down into actions: (1) start an automatic savings plan; (2) look for a starter home where you can rent with an option to buy; (3) speak with a real estate agent so that you know what you'll need. You thus put "buy a house" on your Goals list, but you place your action steps on one of your To Do lists. If your professional goal is to get a promotion, you will want to list the actions you need to take to reach that goal: (1) get appointed to committees; (2) make sure that others know of your successes; (3) take an online or evening course that will give you more credibility.

I do not believe that we ever set goals that are too high. Rather, we often allow too little time to reach them.

—Patricia Hemphill (1992)

In both cases—the house and the promotion—there will be a number of steps you need to take. As you think of them, add them to your list. You can have long-term goals (find your birth parents, volunteer in a needy area of the world, learn to speak Spanish, take blues piano lessons) or short-term goals (put your photographs in albums, start a book club, lose five pounds).

▶ *Subscriptions.* Alphabetize all your newspaper, magazine, and journal subscriptions in one list, along with the date you subscribed or renewed, what you paid, and when the subscription will expire. How many times have you been surprised to receive a renewal notice, but didn't have the time to hunt up your check or credit card records to see if or when you paid? Because magazines sometimes send renewal notices many months in advance, it's difficult to know when it's time to pay.

▶ *Calls.* Unless you have many calls spread out over time or regular follow-up calls, you probably don't need to make a list. It's more likely that you have a few calls that show up on your Today list. You can also add a call to your Dates list; for example, if a friend has recently had a tragic death in the family, you might make a note at weekly or monthly intervals to "call Pat, 522-1555."

▶ *Errands.* Again, unless you consistently have many errands to run, you might not need this category. Some errands might show up on your Today list, and the others on your General list.

▶ *Deductible Expenses.* You'll have a system for keeping tax receipts. But if you're self-employed, you might want to keep a running list of smaller expenses—postage, long-distance phone calls, reference books, subscriptions, and membership fees, as well as a record of miles driven for business purposes:

- 1/15 postage for Vickery report: $14.35
- 1/20 70 miles to/from Statton meeting
- 1/21 online marketing subscription, 1 yr.: $29.99

▶ *Charitable Deductions.* Indicate the name of the organization, how much you donated or what the in-kind donation consisted of, the date, and whether you have a receipt or other proof of donation.

▶ *Numbers.* You might be glad of a secure list of all the numbers in your life. This particular list could be kept on your desktop hard drive, but it might not be entirely safe on a laptop or in your regular notebook. Be very sure this list is in a safe place, however. It holds the keys to your entire life. Among the numbers you might want to keep handy are

- Social security numbers for you and for family members
- Locker combinations
- Passwords for websites
- PINs for ATMs
- Passwords for alarm systems
- Access codes for picking up phone messages
- 800 numbers for your credit cards in case they're lost or stolen
- Your medical insurance ID numbers
- Your driver's license number
- Your bank account numbers

You might also keep important birthdays if you don't have a separate list, or clothing sizes for family members if you often buy for them. Once you have a Numbers list, you'll know what goes on it.

▶ *Projects.* When you have a big project at work or at home, break it down into the smallest possible steps and list them here. This is where eating an elephant one bite at a time is a useful concept. You can further break down your project list into Calls you need to make, Tools you need to assemble, Information you need to have, People you need to speak with, and Dates by which various sections of the project need or ought to be completed.

▶ *Other.* Depending on the way you live, you might benefit from other lists:

- Books or items lent to others
- Books to read
- Holiday card lists

- Movies to see/rent
- What to take in case of a fire
- Travel packing list
- Camping packing list
- To do before leaving on vacation
- Local restaurants and sightseeing information (if you have many guests)
- Short list of emergency or often-needed phone numbers
- Dates when family or colleagues are out of town, having surgery, or otherwise need to be considered
- Random thoughts (invention ideas, a topic you want to research for your own amusement, a word to look up in the dictionary, a joke you just remembered)

When Do You "Do" Your Lists?

Once a day, you must draw up your Today list—either the night before Today or first thing in the morning of Today. The Today list is a daily habit. It ought to take no more than a couple of minutes. If something carries today's date, it's obvious that you put it on your Today list. Look through your tickler file and through your other lists to see what's important or becoming urgent, and add that. After the first couple of weeks, your Today list will practically write itself.

As for your longer list, find out what works for you. Some people run their eyes down their list every day, making sure that they aren't missing anything. If you're a little on the compulsive side, you'll be, like Santa, "checkin' it twice." If you're more relaxed, you might need to check in only once a week for a few minutes.

List making and list maintaining take astonishingly little time. Once you get the outline done, you just put things into their proper category, move up the ones that need to be done today or this week, and keep an eye on the rest.

Tips

▶ Ranking the items on your list is almost as important as making the list. Not all the items on a list are of equal value. "Get gas," "hire assistant," and "call police about vandalism" call for very different responses from you. On the one hand, if you're about to run out of gas, you know which item has to be taken care of first. Getting gas is not at all important in the overall scheme of things, but it is rather urgent. Hiring an assistant is important and will probably be time-consuming. On the other hand, it can wait a few minutes. Try to balance the things on your Today list that are urgent with the things that are important.

What's nice about a list is that you get to make it before phones start ringing, people interrupt you, and unexpected urgencies pop in the door. In the midst of chaos, you can always take a look at the list and be pulled back to the center, where you know what has to be done today. In general, time-sensitive items get tackled first. Your priorities will keep shifting, but as long as you have the list in front of you and one or two quiet minutes to study it, you should be able to isolate the item or items that need you right now.

> *A peacefulness follows any decision, even the wrong one.*
> —RITA MAE BROWN (1983)

▶ Organizing your life is based on decision making. Does this tool go in this pile or that pile? Should I do this first or that first? If you hate making decisions, organizing is going to be especially rough for you. You might have to make a few bad decisions ("What's the hammer doing in the screwdriver drawer?") because, for all but the most critical issues, it is better to make some sort of decision than to waffle for hours or days or even weeks.

With practice, your decision-making skills will improve and you'll get the relief that comes from making a decision. A simple way to teach yourself to make decisions is to break the process down into five steps:

• Define the problem ("Where does this file go?").

• See what choices are available to you ("It could go in the C file for "Car" or the S file for "Subaru").

- Evaluate the choices ("Wait a minute—why are there two files for the car?").

- Choose a solution ("I'm going to collapse these into one file called, hmmm, I think I'd look under 'Car' because we might not always have the Subaru").

- Do it.

Although oversimplified, the basic steps should work for most decisions. Once you know that your weak spot is decision making, you can find ways to help yourself over the hurdle.

> *No matter how much information you collect, no decision comes with guarantees.*
> —MADELINE MARIE DANIELS
> (1983)

▶ Refer to your list to match a task with (1) the amount of time you have available, (2) your level of energy, (3) the tools you have available, (4) the related chores you're doing, and (5) wherever you are at the moment. If you're at the office and you have 10 minutes before an appointment, check your list to see if there are any 10-minute chores on it. Or, give 10 minutes to one of the bigger jobs. If you've reached your stupid time of day (doesn't everybody have one?), make phone calls or clean out a desk drawer. If you've got your screwdriver out, check the list to see what else you might need to fix. If you have to pick up a child and might end up waiting, take along a report you need to read. Your list offers you a range of tasks to choose from. Remember, too, that you can always use those 10 minutes to shut your eyes and zone out. Lists aren't meant to turn you into an Energizer bunny.

▶ When drawing up your list for the next day, single out the two or three items that absolutely must get accomplished.

▶ Examine your lists according to the 80/20 rule. Which 20 percent of the items are taking up 80 percent of your time?

▶ Just about everything these days is a piece of information that you may need to respond to. When the phone rings, the mail arrives, a colleague leaves a report, your daughter says she needs tap shoes, your son has a chess tournament coming up, or your nondriving mother makes a doctor's appointment, or when almost anything crosses your desk, your view, or your path, you need to made additions to your list.

► Check your list carefully to see if any chores can be simplified, delegated, made routine, or deleted altogether. Get into the habit of questioning yourself: Do you *need* to do this? Do you *want* to do this? Is this something you feel you *should* do? If so, why? Where is the "should" coming from? It's clarifying to know whether you're doing something because you want to or because you have to or because someone else is making you feel that you should. And ask the further questions: Is it necessary for me, personally, to do this, or could someone else do it? Just because I've done this for years, does that mean I have to keep doing it?

► List-making software, including downloadable free software, might be right for you. It's not for everyone, but it's worth a look. Google "to do list software" and you'll find dozens of attractive, helpful programs, ranging from simple to complex. Be sure to read users' comments to see what they like about each program so that you can choose the one that works best with the way you think. Some of them work with your e-mail service so that it's convenient to add items to your list from something you just learned from an e-mail.

► If your biggest problem is failing to check your list often enough, you might use a to-do-list software site as your homepage, so that every time you log on to the Internet, you see it.

► Once you've planned a conference or a wedding or a family reunion, extract all your to do items from your notes and add another sublist to your lists. You've already done the hard part; it doesn't hurt to save that list for the next similar event.

► Keeping a daybook or, better yet, a computer file with notes for each day's date is a nice complement to your To Do list. For one thing, it's extremely helpful to take notes on everything you do each day. You can then look back and see that, indeed, you did return a call. You can find the confirmation number for an order you put through—and from the date you ordered it, you can see that it ought to have arrived by now. You have the telephone number of someone you called, plus notes on what was said. You know when you had your oil changed, your cholesterol checked, and your annual review completed. It works like this. As soon as you do something from today's To Do list, move that item to your daybook (basically, your "done" book). It's the same as crossing or checking it off, but you now have a record under today's date that it was done. If your task was to "renew newspaper subscription," you move that item to your daybook for today's date, and you add the expiration date and how much you paid for it. If you don't have a separate list with all your subscriptions, you might at some point want to know just when and what you paid.

> *Out of the strain of the Doing,*
> *Into the peace of the Done.*
> —Julia Louise Woodruff
> (1910)

► If you live with other people, some lists need to be common property—for example, the shopping list. Keep a list available in an accessible area (kitchen bulletin board, on the refrigerator, by the phone) and transfer that list to your central shopping list regularly, leaving a clean sheet of paper in its place.

► A family calendar—a big one—to track the activities that others need to know about is a necessity. No one has to list work events unless they involve travel, an evening meeting, or something that impinges on family time. But all scheduled activities for children (dental appointments, soccer games, school conferences), all activities of parents that take place during family time, and all communal events (the family is invited to dinner by the grandparents) should be listed. This calendar is critical to the smooth functioning of people who live together. You can embroider on the basic idea by giving each person a different-colored marker for their events, by keeping sticky notes nearby so that someone can question an activity ("Jack, do you need to be at practice at 6:30 a.m. or p.m.?"), and by a quick review of the calendar in the morning to make sure there've been no changes to the day.

▶ When you add to your tickler list to have lunch with Chester on April 5, at the same time make a note for April 4: "Call Chester to confirm, make reservation at Nipote's, find the books you borrowed from him." If you make an appointment with a specialist on a certain date, make a note a few days before to call your internist for your records. The point is to be good to yourself, to be your own assistant, thinking ahead to what you'll need to do and know.

> *A schedule defends from chaos and whim. It is a net for catching days. It is a scaffolding on which a worker can stand and labor with both hands at sections of time. A schedule is a mock-up of reason and order—willed, faked, and so brought into being.*
> —ANNIE DILLARD (1989)

▶ An advantage to lists is that they allow you to be mulling over upcoming tasks and activities. An old Marine adage, "Plan early, plan twice," was adopted to keep plans from getting set in concrete too soon. Before you get to a task, it's good to brainstorm and indulge in a little divergent thinking. You'll be surprised at some of the elaborations your mind will toss out to you about this task or that event after you've seen it on your To Do list for a while.

▶ Watch yourself for a tendency to look at your list and repeatedly not "see" some of the more ornery tasks. It's a human thing. Nobody likes the hard jobs, and the brain is happy to cooperate in skipping right over them. Allied to this is the false security of thinking you accomplished a lot because you've been crossing things off your list like crazy . . . but they are all trivial chores. That's good. They need to be finished, too. But just keep some sense of how much time you're giving every day to the truly important tasks.

▶ It may or may not suit your way of looking at things, but if you find yourself feeling overwhelmed, look at your list and make from it a short list of the tasks that are making you feel overwhelmed. Try to figure out what's overwhelming about them, and what you can do about it.

► The only good list is a list that works. Every once in a while, ask yourself if your lists are making your life easier or more difficult. Do more of what's working and change what's not working. But don't give up. Some day you're going to be approaching bewildered strangers and saying, "Listen. The answer to the good life is the list."

CHAPTER 4

Getting Started

*You plant a garden one flower at a time. … You
write a book one word at a time, clean a closet
one shelf at a time, run a marathon one step at
a time. If you feel defeated by some large task,
get your spade and dig the first hole.*

—JEANNE MARIE LASKAS (2007)

M ary Kay Ash, who created the Mary Kay Cosmetics empire, once
said, "You can eat an elephant one bite at a time."

Where you take your first bite depends on your temperament. To
begin organizing some part of your life, choose a task that, when finished, will give you a sense of victory and satisfaction . . . and the desire
to do another task.

First Step

▶ Begin with the area that causes you the most irritation: a closet? your
desk? the garage? Break that area down into its smallest components.
A closet could be divided into overhead shelf, shoes, suits, shirts,
purses, and ties. Divide the desk into surface, middle drawer, each of
the side drawers, and file drawers. The garage includes car-related
items, hand tools, power tools, lawnmower and yard implements,

perhaps trash and recycling containers. Choose the segment that bothers you the most and start there.

▶ Or, start with the easiest task you can find: your briefcase, the silverware drawer, the glove compartment, your e-mail address book, your jewelry box, your CDs, the closet under the stairs, the music in the piano bench, your estimated taxes file, or one kitchen counter.

▶ Select an area that can be left in process while you work or live around it. If you isolate your paper files or your office supplies and work only on them, you will be able to continue using your desk. If you work on your recipe collection or the guest room or the front hall closet, the rest of the house can still function normally.

▶ In the beginning, set a timer for 15 minutes or half an hour and work on a task only until the buzzer goes off. You may get involved and want to continue, but you're also free to leave the job without feeling guilty because you've done what you set out to do. Linda Barnes admitted, "Guilt is the major motivating force in my life." If that works for you, fine. But Lillian Hellman's two cents' worth is, "Guilt is often an excuse for not thinking." Or not doing. The object of setting a timed goal is to leave your organizing work feeling good about what you've done, not guilty about what you haven't done.

▶ If none of these methods work for you, go online and Google "organizers." Entire companies are devoted to your organizing needs. If you have not yet been dazzled by the plethora of handy items, the specificity and usefulness of what you see will seduce you. However, do not—no matter how tempted you are—buy anything just yet. Familiarize yourself with what's available, bookmark helpful sites, and make notes of what you like. Then, when you're organizing your business cards, your stacks of reading, your shoes, or your linens, you will know precisely what, and how many, you need. Do your sorting and make your piles first. Then you can order those boxes, shelves, hooks, dividers, and hangers. If you want to visit a brick-and-mortar organizing store, you'll be inspired by all the things that are available to help you. But again, don't buy just yet. Until you're halfway into an organizing task, it's never clear what the ideal solution might be.

Purchase something only if it makes you positively wild to get at the closet or desk cleaning.

▶ If you're an extrovert, it may help to work with someone else. Invite a friend, spouse, or child to share the fun. However, since you're the one who will be maintaining whatever you organize, be sure that it's you who decides what goes where and in what order so that retrieval will be easier.

▶ If you still have trouble getting started, remember that "any system left to itself will probably, over time, become more disordered rather than more ordered." As Eric Abrahamson and David H. Freedman said, "Things generally don't neaten themselves." You know that, of course, but try to create a mental picture of the disorder that you're looking at today when it is two weeks, five months, or one year later. Your only question remains the one once posed by the wise Rabbi Hillel, "If not now, when?"

Second Step

▶ After choosing a starting place, clear out, take out, and lay out everything in the small area you're working on so that you can see it all. If there are other items in your office or home that belong to that category of items, go get them. Everything that falls into a certain group (tools, stationery, photo albums, medicine cabinet) needs to be in one place.

▶ Start making piles of like items: all the letterhead here, all the notecards there, the postcards in another pile. All the cans of soup here, the beans there, the spaghetti sauce elsewhere.

▶ Make one of four decisions about each item:

1. To keep it—this item goes back in its place (drawer, cupboard, closet, or shelf).

2. To throw it out—this item goes in a large, heavy-duty garbage bag.

3. To give it to someone—this item goes in the Give-Away pile.

4. To think about it later—this item goes in the ? pile because you're not sure where it belongs or what you want to do with it.

Items that you haven't touched in months or years go into the Give-Away pile or, if they're damaged or have passed their expiration dates, into the garbage bag.

> *Just clearing one drawer can open up your heart and mind to new possibilities. You will immediately feel a sense of relief and will have more energy to continue the process.*
> —JAYME BARRETT (2003)

► All you really need to get started is a couple of heavy-duty garbage bags and some sticky notes and a marker. Later, when everything is in its proper pile and you can visualize how the items that belong in this area will be arranged, you can determine what you need in the way of additional shelving, see-through storage boxes, hangers, labels, jars, bins, or specialized organizing elements.

► Thoroughly clean whatever shelves, closet, pantry, cupboard, or box you have emptied.

► Assess how you use that closet, those files, or the pantry. What is a logical ordering of the things you keep there? Arrange items according to where it's easiest and quickest and most logical for you to find and use them. Thus, one person might keep all bathroom cleaning supplies in the kitchen because all the other cleaning supplies are there. Another person might have a set of cleaning supplies under the sink in each bathroom. A third person, with young children, might keep all the cleaning supplies on the top shelf of the pantry. There is no one right way to organize, only the way that is right for you. Think about how you operate, how you will be using the items, and when you will be needing them.

Group like things together. Seldom-used items belong in the least-accessible areas; often-used items should be in the front. It's worth a few extra minutes of your time to play with the arrangement. After you finish, you may realize that something you often reach for isn't accessible. Arrange and rearrange until you are satisfied that your trips to this closet or file will always be happy ones.

► You know what to do with the garbage bag. Place the Give-Away group of items near the door so that when you are leaving, you can take away anything that can be delivered to the appropriate person on your route. The ? items should be placed out of the way. As you continue to organize other areas of your life, more items will join this pile. It will be much easier to deal with these questionable items once you've been through everything.

► To review, then, these are your beginning steps:

- Choose an area or organizing project to work on.
- Lay everything out on the floor, if possible.
- Arrange the items in four piles: Keep, Toss, Give-Away, and ?.
- Clean the area you've cleared out.
- Replace the items being kept in the order that's most convenient for you.
- Take out the garbage bag, and put Give-Away items near the door.
- Place ? items out of the way temporarily.

Part Two

People and Time

CHAPTER 5

Dealing with People

*Have you ever noticed that life consists mostly of
interruptions, with occasional spells of rush
work in between?*

—Buwei Yang Chao (1947)

Unchecked, the people in your life can hijack your entire day with phone calls, drop-ins, "quick" questions, e-mail, correspondence, text messages, favors, commitments, visits, breakfast meetings, lunches, dinners, school conferences, and so on.

We certainly want and need people in our lives. And often there's no one person to blame for our lost days. Most of us are blessed with too many people in our lives, too much of a good thing.

"Dealing with people" can refer to managing a sales force, teaching a college course, interacting with family members, or persuading an audience to enroll in your insurance plan. This chapter, however, focuses narrowly on how to respond to people in such a way that you can remain organized, effective, and courteous.

The Telephone

Not much has changed. It's up to you to decide whether the telephone is your friend or your worst enemy. The average American spends about 40 minutes per day on the telephone. If you're spending much more than this, you might examine where your telephone time goes.

Tips

▶ Never answer the telephone. Use voice mail or an answering service or machine, or have an assistant take messages. (Caller ID allows you to take a call you're expecting.) If you test-drive this strategy for several weeks, you will note an increase in productivity. (And don't feel bad—many people prefer leaving a message to speaking with an actual person.)

The interruptions of the telephone seem to us to waste half the life of the ordinary American engaged in public or private business; he has seldom half an hour consecutively at his own disposal—a telephone is a veritable time scatterer.

—BEATRICE WEBB (1898)

▶ Return all calls once or twice a day (perhaps before lunch or before quitting time or dinner, times that provide a natural excuse for keeping calls brief). The person who makes the call generally controls the conversation, which means that you can determine its length.

▶ When appropriate, get the other person's direct telephone number, so that you don't have to go through a third party.

▶ Your voice mail, answering machine, or assistant should state clearly when you will return calls—for example, morning calls before noon and afternoon calls before leaving the office. When you are out of the office, your message says that you will return calls on such-and-such a date. If you use an answering machine, alert callers if their response time is limited ("You have 90 seconds to leave a message"). Tell people the best time to reach you, for example, "after 4:00 p.m."

▶ Before making a call, jot down or note mentally the points you need to cover. While you are on the phone, take notes on the conversation.

After hanging up from each call, enter in your computer daybook the name of the person called and the salient points discussed. We think we'll never forget certain things. The only thing that is certain is that we will forget some of what we said and when we said it. Be nice to yourself: take notes.

▶ When you simply need to leave information or ask a question and don't need to speak with the person, call after hours and leave a message on voice mail or an answering machine.

▶ When you want to leave a short-winded message with a long-winded person, put it in an e-mail.

▶ If phone time is a big part of your day, buy headphones. Spend a little extra time and money to get a set that will make your life easier.

▶ If you choose to answer the phone, say, as soon as possible, "How may I help you?" or "What can I do for you?" or a casual "What's up?" If you're a naturally genial individual, repress the urge to wax friendly: "How are you?" or "What's new with you?" People like you receive more than your share of phone calls for a reason. If you need to cut back on your phone time, ask yourself if you need to be über-friendly with *everyone*.

▶ Sales and fundraising calls can be stopped by listing your home or cell phone number on the National Do Not Call Registry. Either visit http://donotcall.gov or call 1-888-382-1222. As of February 2008, once you register, you will remain on it permanently. Telemarketers, surveyors, and fundraisers can call those who have had business contacts with them, so you may still receive unwanted calls. If you do, say—in these exact words—"Put my number on your don't-call list." According to Federal Communications Commission (FCC) regulations, once you've said this sentence, the telemarketer is prohibited from calling you again for 10 years.

▶ Call-waiting is helpful when you are indeed waiting for a specific call. In that case, alert the person you are speaking with that you're expecting a call and may have to hang up to take it. Then, if you need to interrupt your call, the other person understands. In general, the advantage of call-waiting is that you can continue to talk, knowing that instead of a busy signal, the second caller is getting your voice mail. If you are the one who is on hold while someone takes that second call, call-waiting is a nuisance and a time-waster. Advice columnist and author Jeanne Marie Laskas says, "I am anti call-waiting. I think it's the rudest invention since the burp." For those who insist on using call-waiting, this is what she insists upon: "If I am put on hold, it's quite all right for me to hang up and wait for the person to call me back after he or she has finished the other call." You may go and do likewise.

▶ Telephone issues in a home office are stickier because many people seem to think that "working at home" is not the same as "working." You, more than most, need to depend on caller ID and return calls only at certain times of the workday.

> *Hi, this is Sylvia. I'm not at home right now, so when you hear the beep . . . hang up.*
>
> —NICOLE HOLLANDER (1983)

▶ Most of the same telephone principles apply to cell phones. However, many cell phone users seem to believe that the ringing or vibrating of a cell phone has priority over every other activity and human being in the vicinity. Calls are naturally prohibited in meetings and at public events, but often a friendly colleague or good friend will take a call while you're standing there in mid-sentence, a third party to an unwanted conversation, wasting your time. If at all possible, leave the person and return to your desk, go to another room, or pick up some work and get busy. Afterward, depending on your relationship with the person, explain that you've lost your train of thought and need to get back to whatever you were doing or tell people bluntly that you barely have time for your own calls, let alone theirs.

How to Cut a Call Short

No matter what you do, a particularly persistent person may continue to talk until your deodorant gives out and your ears are twitching.

You often know in advance who these callers are, so immediately say something like:

- "The next two minutes are all yours, and then I've got to run."

- "I've got exactly three minutes—will that help, or would you rather call back?"

- "I have a minute now, but if it takes longer, I'll have to call you back."

- "I have a meeting in five minutes, and I still have to put some papers together. Can I do something for you in that time?"

- "Hi! I have someone in my office just now, but if I can answer a quick question, I'd be happy to."

- "Can you tell me about it quickly? I have to run."

- "I've got to pick Sam up in a few minutes, but tell me why you called."

- "Actually, I just have a minute. Is that enough, or shall I call you back?"

- "I'm up against a deadline. Can it wait until tomorrow?"

- "I'm working to a really tight deadline today. Is there something I can do for you fairly quickly?"

- "Someone's just coming in for a meeting. May I call you back?"

- "We're about to sit down to dinner. Is there something we can settle quickly?"

To end a call, try one of these lines:

- "All right, then, that seems clear enough. I'll get on it right away. Good-bye."

- "Thanks for your call. I've made a note, and I'll call you as soon as I know anything."

- "My boss just walked in. I've got to go."

- "Uh-oh, meeting time. I've got to run. Thanks for calling."

- "I'm going to be late for an appointment if I don't leave now."

- "I'm sorry I don't have more time to talk just now, but we'll catch up next time."

- "I hope I'm not rushing you, but I've got a meeting."

- "I won't keep you. I know you're busy."

- ▶ "Is there anything else we need to talk about before I head out for my meeting?"
- ▶ "I was going to tell you about . . . but, no, I see I've got to run."

If you can interrupt yourself (as in the last example) rather than the other person, it makes your ending the call more plausible and tactful.

Sometimes you dread returning a call because it always ends up taking at least 20 minutes. If you can't e-mail the person with an adequate response, begin your conversation with something like, "I just have a couple of minutes, but I wanted to get back to you." And then, after a couple of minutes, indicate that your time is up.

If you are seriously bedeviled with telephone calls from people you either don't choose to or can't bear to discourage, you might try something a little underhanded that is, however, effective when used judiciously. Tiny telephone refrigerator magnets sound like real phones when they ring. When a conversation has outlasted your patience, tap the nearby magnet and the person on the other end will hear a ringing phone. Say, "I hope you'll excuse me, but I should take this call." You can't overuse this strategy, but only you know how desperate you become at times with the long-winded.

The Doorbell

Whether the drop-in is a colleague at your office door or a friend on the doorstep, drop-ins can be inconvenient. Some people relish unexpected visitors. However, for those who are in the middle of a thought, on a deadline, or on their way out the door, it's an inconvenience. (Whenever Dorothy Parker heard the telephone or the doorbell ring, she used to say, "What fresh hell is this?")

> The fact is, both callers and work thicken—the former sadly interfering with the latter.
> —GEORGE ELIOT (1852)

Prevention being superior to cure, it's easier to head off drop-in visitors than it is to get rid of them once they've accessed your work area:

- ► Place your desk so that it can't be seen from the doorway, so that your back is turned to the door, or in some other way that would discourage opportunists passing by.

- ► Let it be known around the office that you're friendly after lunch but tend toward the owlish and growlish at other times.

- ► Don't keep an extra comfortable chair in your office. If you do, keep it full of files and books, and do not offer to remove them for anyone except someone you want to sit there.

- ► Keep a huge clock in plain view in your office.

- ► Shut your door and post a positively worded sign ("Please come back at 3 p.m.") rather than a negatively worded one ("Don't bother me.").

- ► If someone follows you into your office, whatever you do, don't sit down. This takes a little getting used to, especially if you're a kindly soul, but it is often necessary.

- ► Pre-sign delivery slips or take care of routine office matters ahead of time so that you aren't interrupted for them.

- ► When you're at home, remember that there's no law that says you have to answer the doorbell. Rita Rudner says, "My father was never very friendly. When I was growing up, I thought the doorbell ringing was a signal to pretend you weren't home." If you have been spotted in the front yard, there's not much use in dashing inside and barring the door. But if you're in the back of the house or upstairs and don't feel like answering it, don't.

If you are still interrupted by a drop-in visitor, minimize the delay in whatever you are doing with one of these strategies:

- ► When you see someone coming, open the door before the person reaches it, and explain that you're on your way out.

- ► Stand immediately and walk toward the person. In a home office or family situation, when you do not want to be interrupted, remain in the entryway or near the door.

- ▶ Greet the person enthusiastically ("I'm so glad to see you"), followed by an immediate "but" ("It's too bad, but I have only a minute. What can I do for you?"). Do not say, "How are you?" as that is a time-honored signal for a friendly get-together. Because of your smiling welcome, you will be allowed to put the person off without harming your relationship. (Whenever you have to say no, begin by saying something positive.)

- ▶ Cut the visit short by saying, "When would be a better time to talk about this/to see you?" or "We need to talk about this, but I can't manage it now."

- ▶ When your time is up, walk toward the door or, in extreme cases, look at your watch (you probably don't need to shake it by your ear) and say, "Thanks for stopping by" or "I guess that'll do it, then. Thanks for letting me know" or "I'm sorry, but I must finish something before I can get out of here tonight."

- ▶ Greet the person; pick up your purse, briefcase, coat, or jacket; and say, "I'm on my way out." And then walk the person through your office door or to their car.

- ▶ Glance at your watch every few minutes. When the other person notices, say something like, "Sorry, but I'm on a short leash right now."

- ▶ Look at your watch and stack some papers together, saying, "I have four minutes before I need to leave. Will that do?"

- ▶ "Someone's expecting a call from me. Can we do this another time? Unless it's something quick . . . ?"

People need to see you throughout the day. Your challenge is to balance your need for quiet time or work time and your need to hear what people have to tell you or ask you. Study your day and see if parts of it lend themselves to quiet time while other parts seem to be people time.

If you keep track of those who interrupt you, you'll find that a very few people are responsible for most of your interruptions. Work on those few. You might mention that an e-mail suits you better than an in-person visit. No one is suggesting that you tell people you have trouble concentrating, and that interruptions ruin your whole day. On the other hand, you might.

E-mail

Does it sometimes seem to you that the latter are the very people who interrupt you so often? If they're not stopping by your office or telephoning you, they're filling your e-box. The people who actually do all the work tend to limit unnecessary visits, calls, and e-mails. (In all fairness, James Tiptree, Jr., pointed out, "There're two kinds of people—those who think there are two kinds of people and those who have more sense.")

> There are, broadly speaking, two kinds of workers in the world, the people who do all the work, and the people who think they do all the work.
> —STELLA BENSON (1915)

Although exact figures are difficult to come by, as many as 180 billion e-mail messages are probably sent every day. Of those, some 70 percent are spam, or junk mail. (Fun-to-know-and-tell factoid: fewer than 200 people are thought to be responsible for 80 percent of the spam.)

Overwhelmed by our e-boxes, we tend to forget that e-mail has contributed incalculable savings to businesses in terms of time, postage, and work hours. The downside is that any time certain people have a thought, they feel impelled to type it down and hit "send." In the old days, they'd never have bothered to write that small idea down in a letter, stamp it, and mail it.

In the age of information overload, most busy people are frustrated with the amount of e-mail they receive, but they fail to see their own role in the chunk of time that e-mail takes from the day.

If you're unhappy with your present e-mail situation, consider changing the way you respond to it. Most of us have done all we can (filters and blocks) to cut back on unsolicited e-mail, but we still struggle to keep current with the legitimate messages we receive.

Answering e-mails is part of the self-interruption cycle. Whenever we need a little stimulus, a mini-mental vacation from what we're doing, we tend to think, "Hey! I'd better check my e-mail." While we're usually disappointed by what we find there, we nonetheless read through a few and think idly about how we'll respond. Eventually, we'll return to our work, although we have by now lost our tight, edgy focus.

> *E-mail is undoubtedly the world's most convenient procrastination device. How many times before making a difficult call, or starting a challenging project, have you said, "Well, let me just check my e-mail first"?*
> —JULIE MORGENSTERN (2005)

Alternatively, you receive a signal every time a new e-mail arrives. This cuts into your concentration and sets up a little hovering cloud over whatever you're doing ("You've got mail! You've got mail!"). It's hard to receive more than a couple of alerts without figuring that you should see what has come in.

According to an article in the *Los Angeles Times* by Leslie Brenner, a growing number of academics are saying that the need to attend to a constantly beeping inbox is creating anxiety in the workplace, adversely affecting the ability to focus, diminishing productivity, and threatening family bonds. "Behind the e-mail backlash," says Brenner, "is a growing perception that, despite its convenience and everything positive it has brought to work and leisure, the tide has turned, and now once-friendly e-mail is a monster that's threatening to ruin our lives."

Then there's recovery time—the time it takes to get back to what you were doing before you were interrupted—which is estimated at 10 to 20 times the length of time of the interruption. Because of the toll e-mail takes, a few companies have even started a no-e-mail-Fridays program.

Tips

- ► Analyze your day and single out the fewest possible (one to four) specific times of day to check your e-mail. And stick to the schedule. After a week of this, you'll be surprised at how much less frantic and interrupted your day seems. (The worst time of day to check e-mail is first thing in the morning. You can get derailed for hours and end up with no energy for something really productive.)

- ► Turn off the e-mail alert signal.

- ► You'll gain some sense of control if you flip e-mails into appropriate folders as soon as you receive them. Each client or project can have its own e-mail folder. You might have files for photos; family; orders;

bank, bill, utility, and other online statements; even for the friend who loads your box with ridiculous forwards. This keeps your inbox from looking overwhelming, and it allows you to respond to one type of e-mail (Client X) in an organized way. Your friend who needs a life can be responded to at the rate of one e-mail from you per ten from her. Caution: one study found that the more folders you have, the less efficiently you deal with e-mail. Only you know what works for you, but a certain number of designated folders seem to be useful.

▶ If you have several e-mail addresses (business, personal, and one that you use when you know it'll trigger junk mail), you might direct them all to the same in-box so that you don't have to check three e-mail accounts. Gmail, for example, allows you to use its interface to forward all your e-mail to one place. Because you can add accounts, you can even respond to e-mail from a different account through that interface.

▶ Effective e-mails (1) always have a subject line that lets the recipient know immediately what you're writing about; (2) are brief and well spaced (one sentence to a paragraph, for example); ideally, the one-screen message should be able to be read without needing to be scrolled down; (3) tells clearly what you want from the recipient ("no response necessary"; "I need to know before 3 p.m."; "If you don't know this, who does?").

▶ For a week or so, practice replying to e-mails in as few words as possible. You'll come across a few useful stock phrases that can be used often:

● Thanks. I've made a note of it.

● You'll have the report Friday.

● I agree.

● Jerry (ext. 314) can tell you that.

People will get used to your brief e-mails and will probably appreciate them. Once you get into the brevity habit, you can whittle away at your e-mails much more quickly.

▶ Some jolly souls are on a mission to share all the jokes, tearjerking stories, uplifting sermons, political rants, and heartbreaking appeals that they receive with everyone they know. If you have one friend like this, you might be able to survive. Too often, however, there are a dozen such individuals, all sending you pretty much the same thing. You might need to write: "I'm barely able to keep up with my business e-mail and rarely get to anything else. Will you please remove my e-mail address from your mailing list for a while until I get my head above water? Thanks." Or: "I appreciate your thinking of me, but I've gotten so busy that I can't find time to open anything but business e-mails. Will you take me off your mailing list? I'll think of you every time I don't hear from you."

▶ Speed is the most attractive part of e-mailing. It also can lead you to waste time. Check e-mail addresses carefully; systems are unforgiving. It's no use having "only" one wrong letter—it still won't fly. If you have to toggle between "reply to sender" and "reply to all," make your default "reply to sender" so that you don't spend days apologizing for something that was intended for one person but went to your entire list.

▶ Some e-mails need to be saved to hard-drive files or printed out and filed. (It is sometimes company policy to save business e-mails. Check your company's policy.) If most of the paperwork dealing with a certain client, project, or case is in a paper file, print out all relevant e-mails for that file.

▶ Your e-mail address book can be one of your most important possessions if you (1) add complete address, phone, fax, Web site, and other information to each person's "card," and (2) back up or print out the address book periodically.

▶ E-mail software programs are largely underused. You can save yourself a lot of time by spending a little time to understand everything your program can do.

▶ Save time by organizing lists of specific groups. When an offspring is going to marry, you can send a "save the date" e-mail to your "family" group in seconds. When a coworker receives an award, the announcement can be sent to your "department" group. A change of practice time can be sent to your "softball" group. Minutes of the last meeting can go to your "communications committee" group. Regrets can be sent to your "bridge" group. However, many people send jokes, comments, and cartoons to what could be called the "everyone I know in the whole wide world and then some" list. Nobody likes paper mass mailings; we don't like them any better on e-mail.

▶ Sometimes you can give your e-mail address online like this: "mary-doe at email dot com" or "marydoeatemaildotcom." This keeps Web-crawling robots from zeroing in on the "@" or the ".com" and seizing your e-mail address for their spam.

▶ Think twice before hitting "send." Surveys have found that some 20 percent of Americans have sent embarrassing e-mails to the wrong person at work. The consequences can be even more than just embarrassing or time-consuming to mop up; one employee ended up in jail because of the content of an e-mail copied to the wrong person.

▶ One of the problems with e-mail is that some people expect an instant response. After all, they have time for e-mail; you must, too. Part of this problem only you can deal with—shutting off the little voice in your head that says insistently, "Check your e-mail, check your e-mail." Ignore it. The other part of this is the other person. Relatively new software can batch your e-mails and send an automatic message saying that you answer your e-mail only at certain times of day or "X appreciates your e-mail, and will respond later today" or "Thank you for your e-mail. X will be unable to reply until Monday." For one thing, this will eliminate all the e-mails you receive that say, "Did you get my e-mail?"

Text Messaging

Text messaging can be a time-saver when you're using it, but an interruption and a time-waster when other people are texting you. In the business world, texting is still considered a little too informal for most people and completely

> *When you take my time, you take something I had meant to use.*
> —MARIANNE MOORE (1935)

inappropriate for others. If you use it, be sure it's acceptable to your clients, bosses, and coworkers. Because of its limited use in business and your ability to respond or not to social texts, text messaging may not be the biggest interruption in your life. If someone is overwhelming you with messages, see some of the earlier suggestions for reducing them.

Mail

Responding to business and personal mail takes less time than it used to, but it's still a part of the daily routine.

Tips

▶ Open the mail in the same place every day and keep a wastebasket, a shredder, and a letter opener nearby. To save a step in your recycling, two wastebaskets are ideal—one for discarded mail and one for unwanted catalogs and magazines. If you're like most people, the bulk of your mail will end up in one of the baskets.

▶ Before tossing envelopes, be sure all return address information is on the letter or enclosure.

▶ When you open unsolicited credit card letters or blank checks, shred anything that has identifying information on it.

▶ Depending on how you think and work, choose categories for the remaining mail and have a container, basket, in-tray, or other specific destination for each. Place every piece of first-class mail in a group, such as

- Bills and money matters
- Work (urgent)
- Work (later)
- Personal (urgent)
- Personal (later)
- Deal with today
- Deal with this week

- Deal with later
- Not sure what to do with

You shouldn't need more than a couple of groups. Some people simply have two piles: urgent and not urgent.

▶ If you can respond to a letter in two or three minutes, do so. You might jot an answer right on a letter, put it in a clean envelope, address it, and be done with it (unless you need to make a photocopy first).

> *Whenever possible, respond to a letter immediately. The longer you postpone answering, the more lengthy the response needs to be.*
>
> —PAT DORFF (1983)

▶ When possible, it's efficient to devote the half hour following mail delivery to taking care of urgent mail. Another time of day—preferably when your energy is a little low—can be set aside for working on the pile of not-urgent mail.

▶ To cut back on the number of catalogs that you receive, especially duplicate copies, go online to www.catalogchoice.com. There you can ask to be taken off the mailing list for a specific catalog. Some catalogs will deny your request, but this particular site is effective in helping you cut back on at least most of your unwanted catalogs.

▶ Taking a few minutes to cancel subscriptions to magazines or journals that you never seem to get to will save you time in the long run.

▶ On the Direct Marketing Association's website (www.dmachoice.org), you can register to be taken off mailing lists, remove your name from prescreened credit offers, and otherwise reduce the flow of unsolicited mail you receive.

▶ A home office benefits from having a mini-postal center: postage scale, selection of stamps, return-address labels, inked stamps (with date, "Media Mail," or other often-used notices), and a variety of mailing supplies. The U.S. Postal Service can set you up as a virtual post office so that you can print your own stamps and mailing labels, saving you gas and time and trips to a post office (www.stamps.com).

- ▶ Recycling bins or baskets
- ▶ Shredder
- ▶ Stacked inboxes, labeled appropriately ("to file," "urgent," "personal," "bills")
- ▶ Stacking cubes for mailing supplies

Faxes

Faxes waste our time when the pages are so hard to read that we have to resend or request a legible copy. Don't fax anything that's already been faxed so many times that it is nearly illegible. Use the superfine setting when the document has small print.

If you fax often, save time by designing dedicated fax letterhead stationery that serves as a cover letter and also has space for the faxed message.

Faxing unrequested sales-oriented material is never appreciated. For the same reason (the recipient bears some of the cost), faxed thank-you notes aren't popular.

Unless you are expecting a particular time-sensitive fax, check the machine only once a day and deal with all faxes at the same time.

Meetings

At least 25 million meetings take place across the United States on an average day, according to business consultant Gene Moncrief. She believes that about half that time is wasted. Susan Ohanian once wrote, "If enough meetings are held, the meetings become more important than the problem." (And management consultant Patrick M. Lencioni once wrote a book with a pointed title, *Death by Meeting*.)

The length of a meeting rises with the number of people present and the productiveness of a meeting falls with the square of the number of people present.
—EILEEN SHANAHAN (1963)

We seem to have a natural impulse to schedule a meeting as soon as any question arises that can't be answered immediately. Consultants can advise your company on how to plan and carry out more effective meetings. There is even software that can track a meeting and tell you how much it cost in terms of people's time and overhead. However, what can you, as one individual, do about the meetings that take up so much of your time?

Tips

▶ Study every meeting proposal as though it were roadkill. Sure, someone has to clean up the roadkill, but does it have to be now? Does it have to be you? Is there a better way to get the job done? Who really needs to be there? Can you replace a meeting with a memo, a conference call, a group e-mail, or one-on-one chats?

▶ Business travel has become so costly that videoconferencing technology, known as telepresence, is a growing feature for some larger companies. Accenture, a technology consulting firm, estimates that its consultants have used virtual meetings to avoid 240 international trips and 120 domestic flights in one month alone, for an annual saving of millions of dollars and countless hours of wearying travel for its workers. Advances in telecommunications networks, software, and computer processing are also producing less expensive collaboration technologies such as Web-conferencing, online document sharing, wikis, and Internet telephony. Companies of all sizes are beginning to shift to Web-based meetings for training and sales presentations. If this technology hasn't already arrived at your workplace to cut the time and expense of some meetings, it will.

▶ Get members of your department or group to fill out an evaluation. What meetings do they attend regularly? How long do the meetings last? How effective are they? How important on a scale of 1 to 10? If you're the boss person, you can have this done. If you're a worker bee, see if you can get others to join you in requesting an evaluation, followed by fewer meetings.

Executive coach, management consultant, and facilitator Joan Lloyd even suggests canceling all meetings for a month, after which each person writes down which meetings they need and why.

▶ Schedule meetings in other people's offices, so that you can leave.

▶ Set your wrist alarm to go off and excuse yourself when the meeting is scheduled to end.

▶ Set up meetings for the hour before lunch or the hour before quitting time, when people are more likely to want to finish on time.

▶ Unless your corporate culture is greatly attached to the custom, don't serve food or beverages at meetings (attendees can bring their own cup of coffee or glass of water). Food means time spent shuffling about with a cup or plate, people distracted by eating, and the atmosphere becoming too relaxed.

▶ Schedule the most critical items in the middle of the meeting, thus avoiding the distractions of latecomers and settling in during the first part of the meeting and the wandering attentions during the last part of the meeting.

▶ Business coach, consultant, and workshop leader Gene Moncrief says that one of the problems with many business meetings is that they try to accomplish too much. Keep them simple and focused. Another problem she notes is that "too often team members are asked to carve out valuable time for meetings in which they have no real role. 'I talk, you listen' isn't a good format because no one listens. It's BlackBerry time."

▶ When you're in charge of a meeting:

  ● Include only those people who are integral to the purpose of the meeting, or suggest that people attend only the part of the meeting that affects them.

  ● Send an agenda to attendees ahead of time.

  ● Attach any necessary meeting guidelines (start and stop times, time limits for each speaker, responsibilities of the chair).

  ● Make sure that everyone's contribution is heard and appreciated. If a few people tend to dominate the discussion, remind them that you have only a limited time and you'd like to hear from those who haven't spoken yet.

- Select a chair who can follow the agenda closely and keep everyone on task. Issues that are not germane to the meeting's purpose can be noted for discussion at another time or assigned to a subcommittee.

- When appropriate, include time for brainstorming, but format it so that people have quiet time to jot down their own ideas before opening up the floor; this levels the field a little between introverts and extroverts.

- See that complete notes are taken about what was said and decided, and about what individuals are responsible for after the meeting.

- Two to four minutes before the meeting is due to end, the chair should sum up the main points and thank attendees for their contributions.

▶ If you're interested in shortening and bettering workplace meetings, and you're not already aware of Edward de Bono and his Six Thinking Hats work, familiarize yourself with his book of the same name.

Requests

If you're a bright, well-liked, and capable individual, you will be approached with many requests: for your money, your time, your talents, the public use of your name . . . to give speeches, conferences, workshops . . . perhaps to lend your home for an event or your cabin for a weekend. Not saying no often enough is one of the biggest causes of being too busy.

I'm always aware that I risk being taken for a neurasthenic prima donna when I explain to someone who wants "just a little" of my time that five minutes of the wrong kind of distraction can ruin a working day.
—GAIL GODWIN (1986)

Tips

▶ This is where your Won't Do list becomes very useful (see Chapter 3). On this list are all the requests you will say no to, all the activities you're not interested in, and all the people you would rather not spend time with. Let's say that the thought of going to a Tupperware party makes you itch. So does giving speeches, attending workshops, and giving workshops. Unless your job or your life requires you to do these things, they belong on this list.

Claire will tutor second graders in reading, but she will not ever make costumes for the school play. Mel will contribute copies of his books to worthy organizations, but he will not ever participate in a book signing. For years Deena has written checks to five charities that she supports, but she will not give a nickel to someone soliciting on the street or collecting at work for a wedding shower.

You don't need reasons for your choices. What you need is a plan, so that when you are asked to do something, you know immediately whether it is something you like doing and are willing to do or something that you never do. Don't be concerned about people who wonder why or who appear critical of your actions. It's not their business.

▶ Before responding to any request, tell the person that you'll get back to them. Say that you have to think about it, check your calendar, speak with your family, or check office policy. Or say simply, "I'll need to get back to you on that." Always leave some time between the request and your answer. You'll make better decisions and have fewer regrets. It also means that people will know that they can count on you. When you do say yes, you are committed.

▶ If you don't like putting people off, jot down some brief responses to the things on your Won't Do list so that you're prepared. Let's say you have no interest in prizefights, estate auctions, playing poker, stopping for drinks after work, and ballroom dance lessons. The minute a key word pops up in the conversation, start shaking your head slowly and say something like

- "I'm sorry, but I'm not interested."
- "Sounds great for someone, but it's not my cup of tea."

- "Thanks for asking, but I can't."
- "Nope, sorry. I don't indulge."
- "I appreciate being included, but it's a no."

▶ Keep your no simple. Do not offer reasons or excuses or explanations. Stating your reasons gives the other person an opportunity to counter them, and the more you try to defend your position, the weaker your argument will appear. Confine your no to one sentence, and repeat it and repeat it and repeat it.

▶ If you have trouble saying no face to face, call and leave your brief "I can't" on voice mail after hours or send a pleasant no via e-mail.

▶ It may help you say no if you remember that saying yes and then not fulfilling your commitment is unkind and thoughtless. People will not remember how much they liked you when you said yes, but only how angry they were when you didn't come through.

> *It's okay to say no to unwanted social invitations. . . . You will not be banished to the tundra to die alone because you decline an invitation.*
> —Jan Jasper (1999)

▶ If anyone pushes the issue or makes you feel bad, you can either get a little aggressive (say with a frown, "Why are you being so insistent?" or with a smile, "What part of no don't you understand?") or walk away, knowing that any rudeness in the situation is the other person's, not yours.

▶ If you're a go-to person for too many others, you might spend a lot of time each week doing favors for people. In that case, put a limit on the number of times you say yes. If you've already driven someone to pick up their car at the auto-repair shop, if you've already picked up and dropped off dinner for an ailing neighbor, watched a friend's child, and taken your coworker's calls for a day, you might have reached your limit. Your answer when asked for a fifth favor? "I'd really like to help you out, but I can't. Call me again sometime. I'm sorry this isn't possible."

▶ Keep it simple. The best response to someone asking for your time, your talents, or your money is, "I'm sorry, I'm not able to do that." When the person presses the issue, keep repeating, "I'm sorry, I'm not able to do that." It is rarely helpful to give a reason, no matter how sound your reason may be. Even being out of the country at the time of an event doesn't help because some people will reschedule in order to include you. It's nearly impossible to argue against "I'm sorry, I must say

> *"No" is not a four-letter word!*
> —CHRIS COUCH (2004)

no" or "I'm sorry, but I can't do it." Don't even say, "I wish I could, but I can't." You're letting the camel's nose in the tent. The first time you say, "I'm sorry, but I can't help" will be difficult, but it will eventually become second nature. Repeat the same sentence over and over:

- "Company policy doesn't allow that."
- "I appreciate your interest, but I have to say no."
- "I certainly wish you luck, but you'll have to count me out."
- "I don't do that."
- "I have a conflict."
- "I have to say no."
- "I won't be able to help you with this."
- "I'm overscheduled and can't take on anything new for the next two years."
- "I'm sorry, but I can't."
- "I'm sorry, but we never do that."
- "I'm sorry, I must say no."
- "My family and I are not able to help out."
- "Thank you for thinking of me, but I'm not able to."
- "Thanks for asking me, but no."
- "That won't work for me."
- "That's very flattering, but I can't."

- Saying no to your supervisor is a tricky business. Whatever your reason for not wanting to take on a particular job (you're too busy, the job is unpleasant, or you don't feel capable of managing it), you need to find a reason that speaks to the supervisor's interests rather than to yours. How could it serve your boss to give the job to someone else? Consider saying something like:

  - "You know that Battles is waiting for this report I'm working on. Perhaps you could convince them to wait a little longer so I could take on this new job?"

  - "Two people in the department are on vacation and another is out sick. I don't think we could do the kind of job on this that you want."

  - "I'm flattered that you'd think of me for this case, but maybe you've noticed that I've been staying after hours to work on the rest of my caseload. I don't see me meeting the deadline."

  - "You know I've always been interested in that account. But the timing is pretty bad because I'm overloaded as it is."

  - "You know who'd love to get her hands on that project? Did you check with Monica Fratelli?"

People Who Can't Get Enough of You

- *Bosses/customers/clients.* You're understandably leery of cutting off people who are closely tied to your livelihood. However, occasionally you have a boss, customer, or client who takes too much of your time. Prevention is the first line of defense. With a client, let your assistant or voice mail take the message as often as you think you can get away with it. Should someone drop in, you're just on your way out. For a supervisor, if possible, spend time in the lab or the library or making sales calls, leaving a note on your door saying where you are so that you are seen as unavailable but hard at work. When you are trapped, work is always the best excuse—both bosses and clients understand that. Try to have something plausible that needs doing at hand. See some of the previous suggestions for more ideas (no extra chair in your office, for example).

▶ *Coworkers.* When you allow coworkers to take too much of your time, others will assume that it takes two to tango. You will be considered to be as chatty and idle as the other person. So, for your mental health, your ability to get things done, and your job reputation, you must ward off these friendly folks. Sometimes someone has an ostensible reason for interrupting you ("I wanted to leave you a copy of the minutes") but then stays to talk. Either way, you can appear harried and distracted, shuffling papers and saying, "Umm, I'm sorry. What?" Or try:

- "Hey, I really want to talk with you, but not now."
- "Can't stop now. When are you taking a break? I'll meet you in the break room."
- "I've already used up my chat time today. Sorry."
- "I've got to get this in the mail. Can I have a rain check?"
- "Can this wait? I've got to put out a small fire."

This sort of person is clever, though. They'll often come back with, "Really? What's going on? Can I help? What time do you have to have it in? Is this the Trilling deal? Wasn't Frannie supposed to help with that?" Your only recourse at this point is to act crazy. Ruffle your hair, stare at your desk, and then suddenly say, "What? Did you say something?" It's not pretty, but remember that you're not the one who's rude; they are.

▶ *Employees.* It's rare that someone working under you will waste your time with idle conversation. If someone does, you only need to look pointedly at your watch or inquire how their work is coming along.

▶ *Family and friends.* You love these people. You sometimes get mad at yourself for looking upon them as interruptions. The best way to ensure that they don't interrupt you too often when you're concentrating on something or are deeply involved in a task is to make sure that they get enough of you at other times. Prevention is the point. If you're an exceptionally busy person, schedule time with your loved ones—yes, actually put it on the calendar.

When you've taken one of your children to lunch, or when you've just played Scrabble with three of them, they're more likely to honor your request for time to yourself. Some parents spend 15 or 20 minutes at bedtime with each child, doing whatever the child chooses. If you spend an evening with your spouse, friend, roommate, or partner doing something that they enjoy, and you do this more or less regularly, they're not going to be trying to get your attention at inopportune times. Balancing needs in a relationship is beyond the scope of this book, but by spending time with your nearest and dearest (and you probably will enjoy that time), you can save time and arguments and interruptions later on.

▶ *Acquaintances.* When people don't know you very well, they're not sure if you're looking for a new best friend, if you're a candidate for replacing their injured tennis partner, or if you haven't got a life and will welcome any activity that they suggest. You will have to let them know kindly where they might, or might not, fit into your life. After a certain age, some people often have all the friends they can handle. If that's your situation, let acquaintances know that although they saw you at one estate sale, you normally don't have time for anything outside work and family; or that although you were free for a pickup game of basketball, it was a rare outing. When you are trying to convey to a new acquaintance that they should look elsewhere for company, do not return phone calls promptly. Do not get into long chats. Do not tell personal things about yourself. It is more honest to damp down a burgeoning friendship than to drop the person after you realize that you can't keep up.

▶ *Needy people.* Most of us have some needy people in our lives. Someone you respect or someone who you believe deserves compassion seems to call or visit nearly every day and talk rather self-absorbedly for an hour. You can't bear to ignore the person, yet you have things you need to be doing, and you grow irritable and impatient. This is a personal decision, of course, but you might consider supporting one, or at the most two, such individuals as your recognition that you are fortunate not to be in their shoes. Yes, it's time-consuming. But you don't need to listen to every person like this, just to one or two. Draw them out on things they're knowledgeable about so that you feel you're learning something as you go. Award-winning author

Katherine Paterson once said, "As I look back on what I have written, I can see that the very persons who have taken away my time and space are those who have given me something to say." You may not be a writer, but deciding to walk with someone on a bit of their journey may bring you unsuspected benefits.

Courtesies

Finally, don't forget that you may be the interruption or time-waster in someone else's life. Some common courtesies will make you well liked while inspiring people to treat you the same way.

► Begin every phone call with something like, "Am I catching you at a bad time?" or "Is this a good time for you?" For a business call, state your message or ask your question immediately. If the other person has time for small talk, they'll let you know; otherwise, keep it short. Begin personal calls with something like, "Do you have a minute?" or "Are you in the middle of something?"

► When leaving a callback number, say it slowly and distinctly. You might even repeat it at the end of the message. Because it's so familiar to them, people often rattle off or slur over this part of the message.

► Spell your name for people over the phone or in any situation where they might be puzzled.

► Call ahead if you're running late.

► Have up-to-date, crisp business cards handy at all times.

► Instead of stopping by a colleague's office with a non-urgent question, e-mail the question or e-mail a request for five minutes at the other person's convenience.

► If you must stop by someone's home or office, be sure to inquire if they have a minute for you or if it's a poor time for a visit. Be willing to leave if you sense that you've mistimed your visit.

CHAPTER 6

Dealing with Time

Time is the mother and mugger of us all.

—KAREN ELIZABETH GORDON (1989)

eing organized is a matter of using time in such a way that after paying our dues to our work, our family, and our community, we have a little time left over to spend as we wish.

The idea of time has been analyzed by thinkers, doers, and philosophers; struggled with; and sometimes rejected entirely. We tend to think of time in the same terms in which we think of money: make time/make money; waste time/waste money; save time/save money; lose time/lose money. In the United States particularly, time is money, and only money—in certain cases—can buy you time.

Some people's relationship with time is adversarial. They are constantly aware of the minutes slipping by, and they try to wrest a few extra ones out of their day. At the other extreme are those who are at ease with time, believing that all things happen when they're meant to happen, that everything will get done in its own good time. Everyone has the same 24 hours to spend, but the way we look at time can affect whether we feel harried or relaxed as we journey through our days.

If time obsesses you, a few organizing strategies probably aren't enough to remove your time stress. You might profit from thinking seriously about your notions of time and your place in it.

On the practical level, you can avoid the following time-wasters and cultivate the time-savers.

Time-Wasters

Sometimes all it takes is being conscious of what you're doing and why to recognize and avoid the time-wasters.

Multitasking

Are you surprised? For some of us, multitasking never meant much more than playing Free Cell while we were stuck on hold on the telephone. But others of us believed that we could file papers while talking with a client and fold clothes while debriefing our kindergartener. Studies have proved us wrong. Doing two things at once, it turns out, means that both take us longer and neither gets done well. In addition, according to Sue Shellenbarger ("Juggling Too Many Tasks Could Make You Stupid," *Wall Street Journal*), "Chronic high-stress multitasking also is linked to short-term memory loss."

> *Not all speed is movement.*
> —TONI CADE (1970)

Certainly, take papers and journals along to read while you're waiting for an appointment or while you're commuting on the train, bus, or subway. When you're on hold, you can delete unwanted e-mails or download a document. If the person on the other end of the telephone doesn't mind, you can use the speakerphone while doing something rote (stuffing envelopes perhaps). But because multitasking reduces productivity, if you're using the speakerphone while filing, your filing will be slower and less accurate. You're better off concentrating on the person with whom you're speaking and then afterward focusing on filing. If you've telephoned individuals who are multitasking while they are talking with you, you know how irritating and unsatisfying it can be.

One annoying little outcome of multitasking is what happens when you receive a telephone call from a Nonstop Talker. Because it's a friend who's going through a divorce or a parent you honor or a colleague who's been helpful to you, you put up with it. But to lessen the pain, you start playing Hearts or Super Collapse (without the sound) while they're talking. Because you're involved in shooting the moon or exceeding a million points, you let them go on and on. This sets a precedent. The person henceforth knows that they can talk as long as they wish. Their calls become longer and more frequent because you're not giving them 100 percent of your attention. If you were, you couldn't bear it, and you'd find some way to end the call, which means the calls would become somewhat less frequent and lengthy.

Some multitasking works. (1) Keep a tray of items that need to be input into your computer files (business cards, sticky notes with phone numbers you want to retain, the confirmation number for a payment) between the phone and your keyboard. When you are on hold, there's usually enough time to input some of this rote typing, and you'll save yourself the little hiccups in your day of inputting a phone number here and an address there. (2) Exercise while watching movies, walk or bike to work and make it aerobic if you can, garden or do yard work vigorously enough to count as exercise. (3) Watch TV and fold laundry, watch TV and give yourself a manicure or pedicure, or watch TV and sort your tackle box.

A few multitasking routines work; most don't. Examine your habits to see if you're wasting time by trying to do two or three tasks at once.

For the most part, you'll finish more quickly and do a better job if you focus tightly on a task and give it all your attention.

Worrying

Years ago, Corrie ten Boom said, "Worry is like a rocking chair—it keeps you moving but doesn't get you anywhere." Today, time management guru Kerry Gleeson phrases it a little differently: "Constant, unproductive preoccupation with all the things we have to do is the single largest consumer of time and energy."

In between planning and doing is pointless worrying. We accomplish nothing whatsoever by one second or one hour or one month of worry. And this mental squirreling around eats at our concentration and takes up mental space that we need for either accomplishing something else or, if we're lucky enough, refreshing ourselves when we have leisure.

Most important: most of what we're worrying about never happens.

> *Never go out to meet trouble. If you will just sit still, nine times out of ten someone will intercept it before it reaches you.*
>
> —CALVIN COOLIDGE

The solution? Write it down. Make a list of what is preoccupying you. Under each item, note what you need to do to attack that issue. Then, choose one item—no matter how insignificant—and do it. Chipping away at something that worries you—accomplishing even one part of what needs to be done—allows you to stop worrying. You're one step closer to taking care of it.

> *There is usually an inverse proportion between how much something is on your mind and how much it's getting done.*
> —DAVID ALLEN (2001)

It may take some time to conquer the worry habit, but when you do, you will avoid hours of useless anxiety, inattention, and unhappiness over your lifetime.

Thinking is not worrying. Sitting with your feet up on your desk, looking out the window, and mulling over a problem can be useful and productive. Most of us know the difference between thinking ("We could ask for an extension," "I'll ask Harriet to check on other venues," "We should look into a substitute") and worrying ("What am I going to do?" "What if the worst happens?" "What will they think?" "Will I be able to do it?").

> *Stress is an ignorant state. It believes that everything is an emergency.*
> —NATALIE GOLDBERG (1990)

Thinking produces more actions, different actions. Worrying is no more productive than chasing your tail. Let your dog take care of that part of life.

Stressing is just another way of saying worrying, except with a little more noise and a few nervous tics. When you find yourself feeling panicky, determine whether you are indeed in the midst of an emergency. If you are not, sit down and list steps that might take you out of whatever hole you are—or imagine you are—in at the moment. Then choose the smallest step, and take it.

Starting a Task Before You're Prepared

Before you make your first move to write and mail a report, install a new door lock, order new office equipment, lay tile, hire an assistant, plan an event, or replace your old desk with a new one, gather everything you need: tools, equipment, materials, information, and phone numbers. Plan how much time and money you expect the task to require. When necessary, speak first with the people who can help you or who need to be involved. Know what steps you must take to accomplish the task. Break the job into small, manageable bites.

Much can be said of those energetic individuals who see what needs to be done and dive right in. However, all too often, these are the same people who make three trips to the hardware store to pick up what they've forgotten, who remember too late who has their variable-speed drill, who don't call ahead to see if the person they need is available, who forget that they'll need their checkbook, and whose disposition at a variety of these points changes from optimistic and energetic to irritated and angry.

Think through a project on paper, listing everything you'll need to know and have before you begin. Group similar tasks, errands, and equipment. Make your phone calls. Gather your materials. Now you're ready to go.

Not Knowing When to Quit

Most of us have been raised in a "try, try again" culture. Our heroes have modeled stiff upper lips, and they have not given up the ship. None of us likes being called a quitter. And yet . . .

Knowing when you're throwing good money after bad can save you hours, and often months, of fruitless work, anxiety, and money. There are few easy ways to know when a project or endeavor is not worth pursuing. You can, however, get into the habit of questioning yourself frequently. Too many bad feelings, too many negative omens, or too many things going awry are sometimes signals that this particular scheme is not meant to be. Perseverance and hard work aren't effective when your very premise is unworkable. Quitting is sometimes the right thing to do. When in doubt, ask yourself whether you are being persistent or stubborn. Hardworking or hardheaded. Determined or close-minded. Ask several people who are familiar with the situation what they think. You don't necessarily have to adopt their conclusions, but do listen to them.

No one likes to admit failures and mistakes, but sometimes you need to stop while they are still small failures and little mistakes.

Television

According to the A.C. Nielsen Co., the average American watches more than 4 hours of television every day. This amounts to 28 hours per week, or 2 months of nonstop TV-watching per year, or—in a 65-year life—9 full years in front of the television.

Can you imagine what you could do with nine full years?

Millions of Americans are so hooked on television that they fit the criteria for substance abuse as defined in the official psychiatric manual, according to Rutgers University psychologist and TV-Free America board member Robert Kubey. Heavy TV viewers exhibit the following dependency symptoms (two more than necessary to arrive at a clinical diagnosis of substance abuse): (1) using TV as a sedative, (2) indiscriminate viewing, (3) feeling loss of control while viewing, (4) feeling angry with oneself for watching too much, (5) inability to stop watching, and (6) feeling miserable when kept from watching.

On the other hand, "International comparisons show that annual hours spent in front of the tube correlate strongly with annual hours worked. The more a country's people work, the more they watch TV. When you're exhausted, it's easier to curl up on the couch and grab the remote" (John de Graaf, *Take Back Your Time*).

Knowing that you're watching television because you're exhausted may help you choose a better use of that time—a nap, for example (although some clever people turn on the television so that they can nap while giving the appearance of doing something).

If television viewing is your biggest comfort in life and you feel you use it wisely, skip this section. However, if you are uneasy about the amount of time you spend watching television, you might think about trading up.

What else would relax you as much as watching television?

For many people, a book or a magazine is equally restful and leaves you a little smarter than you were when you picked it up. But often there's nothing appealing available. This means you need to do a little advance work: subscribe to a magazine you've always wanted to read; get a library card; order new or used books online. Once you get into the habit of making sure that you have reading material, you're going to be a lot better off at the end of a year than if you'd spent the same amount of time watching television. Smart people start by doing some work-related or self-help reading, with the promise of a treat (a thriller or bestseller) after half an hour of "improving" reading. Keep two piles of books going—the interesting ones and the fun ones.

Most of us could use all the exercise we can get. Again, the problem is forethought and fore-action. The exercise has to be as accessible as the television and almost as entertaining. Put the exercise bike in front of the television and watch movies you've always wanted to see. You could possibly reach the point where you can't wait to get to your exercise so that you can watch the second half of *Plan 9 from Outer Space*. Or get a family member or neighborhood friend to go for an after-dinner lope. You don't need to overdo it. Any exercise is going to do more for you than sitting in front of the television.

If you've ever had an itch to grow bonsai trees or make mosaics or get back to your childhood stamp collection, this is the time for it. Make it easy for yourself: stock up on whatever accessories you need, find a space to dedicate to your hobby, and set up that space so that all you have to do is pick up the stamp tongs or choose your next piece of colored tile.

It takes a little planning to use that television time, but it will gain you hours and hours of time to spend on activities that make you feel more energetic and alive. Some days, getting in that after-dinner walk or reading that magazine may be your biggest accomplishment. You'll fall asleep happier for it.

It doesn't have to be an all-or-nothing proposition. Check the television and cable listings once a week and mark anything that you really want to watch. But turn it off as soon as your show is over instead of picking up the remote to see what else is going on.

Interruptions

The last chapter suggested ways of dealing with people who interrupt you with their drop-in visits, phone calls, and e-mails. But what about that great interrupter . . . yourself?

Yes, you. Most people interrupt themselves frequently throughout the day, but don't recognize or name their behavior as an interruption.

According to Maggie Jackson ("May We Have Your Attention, Please?" *BusinessWeek,* June 12, 2008), "Roughly once every three minutes, typical cubicle dwellers set aside whatever they're doing and start something else—anything else. It could be answering the phone, checking e-mail, responding to an instant message, clicking over to YouTube, or posting something amusing on Facebook. Constant interruptions are the Achilles' heel of the information economy in the U.S. These distractions consume as much as 28% of the average U.S. worker's day, including recovery time, and sap productivity to the tune of $650 billion a year, according to Basex, a business research company in New York City."

Apparently some software help is on the way—programs to rank incoming messages' importance using probability models, to hold messages until users are ready for them, and even one to judge keyboard activity to determine how interruptible you are at the moment.

For most of us, any interruption will do. A few minutes into writing up a contract, you're reminded of a question about liability. You call the company lawyer. Her assistant says that Marian will call back as soon as she gets off the phone. Fifteen minutes later, you're still shuffling things around on your desk waiting for the call.

Tip: When you're in the middle of a task, jot down related questions instead of haring off after the answers. In the case of the contract, insert in the text where the information should go, in brightly colored capital letters, "FIX" or "INSERT NEEDED." When you've put the contract together (a task that takes concentration and time and that is most efficiently done in one piece), you can return and fill in the missing pieces—work that can fit between smaller tasks. It's much better to complete the biggest, most important part of a project than it is to complete the little bits and pieces. Don't interrupt yourself with the latter when you're in the middle of the former.

Or, midway through washing the windows, you think about shining your shoes for a Saturday wedding. Half an hour later, your shoes are shined, along with a couple of other pairs you thought you'd do, and you and your roommate have taken time out for a beer. But now your bucket of vinegar and water looks scummy, the light has changed, and you see streaks on two of the windows you already did. Somehow, you just don't feel like finishing the job.

Tip: Interruptions breed interruptions. If you set out to do a task, have your supplies gathered, and know that there's enough time to do the job, then do it. Tough it out. It takes only a little effort to repress the desire to do something else. If you finish what you start, you'll feel much better afterward.

Peter Drucker, often considered the founder of modern business management, determined that working concentratedly for 90 minutes allows you to accomplish more than you can in twice the time if you are interrupted. He found that 90 minutes is ideal for attention span, focus, and dealing with multiple ideas at the same time.

We can often blame our subconscious, which is only too happy to seize upon the most trivial excuse to abandon the slogging work we're involved in. But self-interruptions can become habitual, so keep scrap paper at hand, and when you find yourself rising from your chair to do something that's unrelated to the job at hand, sit right back down, make a note of your thought, and get back to work. I know, you wanted a break. But this is why it's called work.

Procrastination

Postponing, delaying, or avoiding a task makes us uncomfortable, and we get mad at ourselves. But sometimes, when you can't seem to get to something, it's because your subconscious has problems with it. Our deepest feelings and thoughts are sometimes smarter than what we see on the surface. When you keep putting off a chore—especially if you're generally good about getting things done—give it another look. Maybe there's a downside you're not seeing.

> *Procrastination isn't always a bad thing. For starters, it can keep you from working on tasks that ultimately turn out to be less important than you thought.*
> —ERIC ABRAHAMSON AND DAVID H. FREEDMAN (2006)

Creative people especially know the value of keeping things on the back burner until their ideas are ready to be deployed. The vastly talented writer Virginia Woolf once wrote, "As for my next book, I am going to hold myself from writing till I have it impending in me: grown heavy in my mind like a ripe pear; pendant, gravid, asking to be cut or it will fall."

Procrastination thus serves us well when a task is either ill advised or not yet ready to be approached.

What most of us mean by procrastination, however, is picking up something, putting it down, picking it up again, returning to it later, thinking of something better to do, knowing that we ought to do it, picking it up again, and finally, in a burst of irritation, going swimming or visiting the refrigerator. According to *Psychology Today*, 20 percent of people identify themselves as chronic procrastinators.

> *Sometimes you end up using more energy stressing over your unfinished tasks than you would if you took a few minutes to accomplish them.*
> —JAYME BARRETT (2003)

You could spend some time trying to figure out why you're procrastinating:

- ▶ You're not really committed to the task.
- ▶ Someone else wants you to do it, and you're a little resentful.
- ▶ You don't really know how to do it.
- ▶ You're a perfectionist, and you don't think you're up to speed on this.
- ▶ You fear failure or criticism or rejection.
- ▶ You're overwhelmed by everything else you have to do.
- ▶ There's no deadline, so what's the hurry?
- ▶ It's unpleasant, boring, or too complicated.
- ▶ You just don't feel like it.
- ▶ There's always something else you'd rather do.
- ▶ You don't think it's that important anyway.
- ▶ You don't know how to get started.
- ▶ It seems to be more than one person can handle.
- ▶ Your parents were very strict, so you take every opportunity to not follow orders, even your own.

There's only one cure for this: just do it. You'll have to experiment with this for several weeks before you begin to appreciate the beauty of it. But whenever you start to push something aside to do later, or pick up another, easier task to do in its stead, stop yourself. Tell yourself, "15 minutes." Spending 15 minutes working on the dreaded task will put you in the middle of it. If 15 minutes is all you can do, you are still ahead of the game. But usually, 15 minutes into the job, you are . . . well, into the job. And you are surprised to find that it's not so bad.

With procrastination, the problem often isn't so much that something doesn't get done, because it will get done. You wouldn't have a job or a life if you never finished anything. So it will get done. But the time you waste procrastinating . . . now, that's the issue. You can never recover that time. So if you know you're procrastinating, the least you can do is stop fiddling with the papers, thinking about doing the job, and berating yourself for not doing the job.

Added to the time wasted by procrastination are other costs. If you delay mending a small crack, it will soon be a large crack. If you don't write a six-sentence thank-you note now, you'll end up writing a six-page letter apologizing for the six-month delay, offering excuses, and being about six times warmer and wordier than you would have had to be in the beginning.

Practice saying to yourself "Do it now" and "15 minutes." You'll like the results.

Most of us suffer from a misperception about feeling and doing, about motivation and action. Here's a radical thought: you don't actually have to *feel* like doing something to do it. You don't have to be *motivated* to do something. You simply do it. In the act of doing it, you will feel like finishing it and you will be motivated to finish it. The act of doing something can come before you feel like doing it.

The magic words are "just do it."

Shopping

If shopping is recreational for you, if you truly enjoy it and don't feel guilty about your time in the stores, and if you're not spending the grocery money, you probably don't have a problem. However, if you've decided that you're spending far more time shopping than you'd like, you can cut back in a few ways.

► Keep one central shopping list on your computer or in a notebook. Jotting something down when you think of it is fine, but transfer it to the central list as soon as you can. Arrange the list in categories: grocery, department store, hardware store, pharmacy, office supply store, garden center.

► Whenever you head out of your home or office, call up the list, press "print," and you're ready to go. The idea is not that you need to get everything on your list, but when you have a central list, you can see at a glance which items are critical, which can be combined, and which can be picked up along your route. You also might make an unplanned stop at an office supply store, and, luckily, you've got your list with you.

► Always put items on your shopping list *before* you run out. Never allow yourself to get down to the last ream of copier paper, bottle of shampoo, Band-Aid, printer cartridge, or bag of dog food. In theory, you should never have to make an expensive, time-consuming run for one or two needed items. Most of us learn sooner rather than later how annoying it is to run out of gas, but we're less foresightful about keeping our offices and homes tanked up with supplies, groceries, and everyday necessities. Running out of something is not only irritating but time consuming, especially if it happens often. When you write things down before you run out, you've given yourself a little lead time—there isn't the urgency to buy something immediately. If you do nothing but resolve never to throw on your clothes, get into the car, drive to a drugstore, and buy one bottle of cough syrup, you'll improve your life—because if you're out of cough syrup and someone in the house needs it, you're going to make that trip.

► A corollary to buying before you run out is buying in bulk, an efficient, cost-saving strategy. You have only one set of movements to locate the items, load them onto the counter, bag them, stow them in the car, haul them into the house, unbag them, and shelve them. You take the same steps whether you're buying one bottle of olive oil or two, and you generally save money by shopping at Sam's Club or

Costco or other warehouse-style stores. If you buy five boxes of staples instead of one, you save yourself four sets of motions—to say nothing of the convenience of knowing that you're stocked up. Because it costs more initially to buy in bulk, stagger your shopping. One time, stock up on bathroom supplies. The next time, stock up on condiments and soups. Another time, stock up on CD blanks and software. Rotating groups of similar items helps you remember similar items that you may have forgotten to list.

How do you decide what's good to buy in bulk? Look for things that are fairly important (Band-Aids, #10 envelopes, dental floss), that you would hate to make a special trip to buy, and that you know you will always use eventually. Some things to buy in bulk are

- Canned and bottled foodstuffs
- Paper goods (paper towels, napkins, tissues)
- Postage stamps
- Greeting cards
- Toiletries (razors, shampoo, toothpaste)
- Tapes (cellophane, packaging, masking)

▶ You've probably already discovered the immense savings of time, gas, and effort—to say nothing of being able to shop at odd hours of the day or night—with Internet shopping. When you know what you want, (1) Google it ("boning knife," "inkjet toner ink"); (2) compare prices—there are sites that do this for you, but as they're generally slanted toward a certain group of stores, you're probably better off doing it yourself; (3) then Google "coupon" and the name of the i-store you've settled on. In many cases, you can find an offer for 10 percent off or free shipping. In fact, part of your comparison should include the existence of coupons—although an item at X is more expensive than the identical one at Y, with free shipping Y becomes the less expensive way to go. If you regularly order office supplies from the same company, you can often obtain special discounts, and most items can be delivered to your door within 24 hours.

Time-Savers

Raising your awareness of how you use time—encouraging time-saving habits and discouraging time-wasting ones—can result in serious extra time for you to use as you like.

Identifying the "Right" Time

Not all hours in the day are the same. Your metabolism, circadian rhythm, and biological chemistry have a pattern that is uniquely yours. There are hours when your brain whirs and cranks and spits out ideas that astonish even you. At other times of the day, you can't remember if q comes before or after p in the alphabet. Learn to identify and make use of the ebb and flow of your energy, creativity, and perseverance.

> *One should always act from one's inner sense of rhythm.*
> —ROSAMOND LEHMANN
> (1945)

Many people find that their mental energy and their ability to concentrate are at their peak when they first get up. However, by the time they deal with clothes, hygiene, breakfast, commuting, and reacquainting themselves with what's on their desk, all that "oomph" is gone. You might consider getting up an hour early, going straight to a home desk or a laptop computer, and getting down some of the dynamic thoughts that seem to come to you at this hour. To make up for it, quit work a little earlier or go in a little later, if that's possible.

If you've identified a time of day when your brain is obviously on and clicking away, use it. Set aside that time for your most difficult work, for brainstorming, or for finishing an unpleasant task that you've let sit around. Don't use this productive time to answer the phone or check e-mails or allow yourself to do tasks with immediate but very small payoffs. Do the big stuff.

Your work routine may not always allow you to follow your natural energy rhythms, but even being aware of the times of day when you're hot or cold or in between can help you choose the right work to do at the right time.

During the down time of day, when you want a nap or keep looking at your watch, do mindless work (everyone has a little of this).

The period before nighttime sleep is critical. You can set yourself up for trouble if you use that time to get anxious about everything you have to do tomorrow or to make yourself miserable by thinking about everything you did wrong today. Instead, choose something you're trying to work through—an office problem or a personal problem or even a decision about what color to paint the walls. Tell your subconscious, in whatever words you like, to address this issue while you sleep. Many times you'll wake up in the morning with, if not a solution, at least some terrific ideas about your problem. Knowing that part of you is working, the rest of you can imagine yourself on a beach or flying your own plane or whatever happy scenario will put you right to sleep.

Remember Peter Drucker's advice about working in units of 90 minutes for maximum effectiveness?

The 90-minute span has also been identified as the ideal unit of sleep. You know the difference between waking up alert and being dragged from the depths of sleep caverns. In the first case, you have most likely awakened after $1^1/_2$, 3, $4^1/_2$, 6, or $7^1/_2$ hours of sleep. In the second case, you have awakened somewhere in between.

As all clocks need winding, so all human brains and bodies need to be wound up by sleeping.
—JULIA McNAIR WRIGHT
(1880)

For you, the optimum work or sleep period might be an hour and fifteen minutes or two hours. Your life will go more smoothly if you can identify your own personal pattern and use it. Go to bed at a time that will give you cycles of 90 minutes of sleep.

You might also be more effective if you plan a mix of tasks. After doing a piece of writing, returning phone calls might be a good change of pace. Often, you don't have a choice about what you do next. You are putting out fires, and you take what comes. But when you can alternate sit-down writing work with stand-up filing work with walking-around delivering work, it makes the day go faster, and you tend to do each piece of it more easily.

Choose the Right Time to Stop

When you are working on a long project, take your breaks from it either in the middle of a section or just when the job is getting easy. It's always satisfying, for example, to stop writing when you come to the end of a chapter. But when you come back, you've got the whole next uncertain chapter to get into, and it's going to feel like uphill work. Chances are that you may have to return to your desk several times before you can bring yourself to start.

Starting up from the very beginning is difficult and requires lots of energy. Picking up something that's partly finished is half as difficult and requires half the energy. (That's why writing the first sentence of anything always takes the longest.)

And always, before quitting, know what you're going to do when you return to this spot. If you're in the middle of something, the new starting place will be obvious. But if you do happen to stop working at a logical end point, before leaving your desk, determine the next step and leave yourself a note spelling it out.

Use a Timer

The point of being organized is to feel better, to go to bed at night and sleep the sleep of the just, knowing that you have accomplished a few things that day. One way to make your satisfaction concrete is to use a timer.

When you're working, set the timer for 15 minutes, or for an hour, or for the effective hour and a half. After the buzzer sounds, take a break (or not, if you're in tiger mode). The advantage of a buzzer is that you don't feel trapped—you know that the buzzer is going to go off and set you free. Better yet, you know that you have put in a solid chunk of time working on something that needed doing.

You can also use a timer to limit phone calls, to signal the time allotted for a meeting, or to let you know that it's time to leave for an appointment. Once you have a timer, you'll think of more uses for it and learn to use it as a buddy rather than as a bossy overseer.

Commute Time

If you're driving, your options for using your commute time are limited. Despite more laws mandating hands-free cell phone use while driving, making calls is never a good idea (remember how inefficient multitasking is). You're best off using that time to catch up on the news, listen to a new CD, or put on an audio book.

With today's concerns about gas prices and the environment, your ideal choice is to use public transportation. The advantages are tremendous: time to read or daydream or listen to your iPod, lower auto insurance costs, less wear and tear on your car, and less expense.

Organizing a group to carpool has been a boon for many. Some local newspapers list those looking for people who are traveling their route at their hours. If your paper doesn't do this, suggest it.

Research in your community might turn up a vanpool, which takes carpooling one step further and costs much less. If there are 6 to 17 commuters on your route, each person pays only for gas and for the monthly lease of a van through a reputable corporation that is responsible for insurance, maintenance, and registration. Your auto insurance premiums can be lowered because of your lowered yearly mileage, and you save wear and tear on your own car. Vanpool driving is shared among the commuters (after their driving records have been checked).

Biking to work, when possible, is a money-saver, although it's not much of a time-saver unless it qualifies as your daily exercise. It's also not as safe as it could be, as few communities have the kind of bikeways that make commuter biking both benign and effective.

And then there are feet. Walking is consistently the best all-around exercise, the best present you can give yourself. You might have to make a few adjustments (keep toiletries at work to freshen up after you arrive, for example), but once upon a time most people walked to work. And you don't hear *them* complaining. A two-fer (getting to work and exercising) is always a time-saver and doesn't count as multitasking.

Call Ahead

Get into the habit of verifying all appointments the day before (or at some other reasonable interval). People forget. Airlines double-book. Doctors have emergencies. You'll save yourself irritation as well as time by calling ahead. Be sure anyone you have an appointment with has your number so that they can find you if something comes up.

When you're visiting an unfamiliar store, call ahead to be sure that (1) it's still there and (2) it's open when you expect it to be. If you need to drive more than 15 minutes to purchase something, call first to see if the store has the item you need. Ask the store to set it aside for you. "Let your fingers do the walking."

If you're not already one of the millions whose fingers do the walking on the Internet, never leave home without printing out directions to a business, store, or doctor's office or, if your car has a GPS system, inputting the addresses of the stores you frequent.

Whenever you set up a meeting at an unfamiliar location, get directions right then so that you don't have to call later for them.

When possible, ask for the first appointment or meeting of the day—it's more likely to begin on time. Conversely, try never to get booked on the last flight of the day. If something goes wrong, you're looking at an unscheduled overnight stay.

When you live with other people, double-check every morning to verify any commitments for the day: the time to pick up a child after tennis, the time to meet a spouse for dinner (or the time you're all expected for dinner at home), after-school whereabouts, or an appointment with a financial consultant. From early in your relationships, establish and maintain a be-there policy. Rendezvous with family and friends should be as respected as business meetings.

Deadlines and Tickler Files

Deadlines work for some people, but have no effect (except to increase stress and deepen guilt) on others. Deadlines that you set for yourself feel artificial, and any reasonable person can persuade the person who established the deadline (you) to give them a break. However, most of us respond to natural deadlines (filing estimated taxes, repapering the den before the holidays, turning in your end-of-year numbers, or buying a birthday gift for your mother).

Dates by which you need to do something should all be in the same file, so that you can skim down the list and see if there's anything scheduled for tomorrow, what you need to do next week, and how busy you're going to be next August.

A tickler file is thus any system that helps you see what you need to do in the future ("tickling" your memory). You record or file papers or tasks in one place in your life, a place that you check routinely. You are your own assistant. Few of us have people sticking their heads into our offices to say, "You have a meeting today in the boardroom at four" or "Don't forget to send flowers to the hospital for Gina." You do this for yourself by means of a tickler file.

The three basic ways of organizing these reminders are

- A calendar on which you note every upcoming event or task.

- An accordion file with 31 compartments, one for each day of the month, into which you drop papers or notes to yourself to deal with on that particular day. This doesn't work for most people today because so much of our lives is on the computer and because some items don't fit handily into an accordion file. But if it works for you, go for it.

- A linear computer file; for example:

  Jan. 3: send Dad a birthday card

  Jan. 6: give Dad a birthday call

  Jan. 17: buyer from Nash, Inc., at the office all day

  Jan. 18: ask Jan to look over the Massinol report

  Jan. 25: oil changed in the car

  Jan. 31: Massinol report due

A handy aspect of this is that you can highlight items and move them from this all-purpose tickler file to your file for the week or the day. Get into the habit of checking your tickler file every day so that nothing catches you unaware.

Delegating

The do-it-yourselfer is a great American cultural icon. We're pioneers and cowboys and independent spirits and can-do people. But sometimes working smart means delegating a task. Just because you can do a job better or faster than someone else doesn't mean that it's a good use of your time. The job may not be worth your "best" and "fastest" compared to other, more important things that you could be doing.

Some jobs must be done by you (and incidentally, don't forget that a few jobs that we take for granted don't need to be done at all), but if a job *can* be delegated, it probably *should* be delegated.

In the long run, you save time by spending time. It takes less time to train five people to do some of the work than it would take you to do the work of five people. Train someone to do the job or help another person get up to speed on it. You're being paid to work at a certain level of skill and knowledge. You owe it to yourself or to your company not to do things yourself that someone else should be doing. You don't have to be the whole loaf of bread. Be the yeast.

Delegation means that even though someone else does the job, you're still responsible for the results, so choose carefully. The sharpest knife in the drawer may not meet deadlines. The one who meets deadlines may not have many original ideas. You may not have a choice sometimes, but ask yourself whom you'd rather clean up after if the job isn't done quite to your specifications.

Always give detailed written instructions, and then trust the person to carry them out. Remember that nothing grows very well if you keep pulling up the plant to see how the roots are doing.

If you need to delegate some of your trivial, repetitious work, see if you can give the person a project with some meat on its bones at the same time, something that will—if completed successfully—do the other person some professional good.

Within the family, small children can be taught to make their beds, put away toys, and generally be responsible for their immediate surroundings. Over the years that a child lives at home and does these tasks, a parent can save hundreds of hours of time. But the parent must be willing, very early on, to break each task into steps, to go through the steps with the child, to show appreciation for what the child does, and, most important, to never redo the child's work. If the bedspread (which you have selected because it's easy to manipulate) is crooked or half off the bed, you leave it. Things will get better. And you will both be winners: the child at the independence game and the parent at the time-saving game.

At work, it will be more difficult for you to overlook poorly done, slowly done work, but if you keep in mind the long-term savings in time, you will kindly and effectively reteach the task until you are (mostly) satisfied with it. If you truly have no gift for teaching, see if someone else can teach the task.

Don't be taken in by some people's display of inadequacy. The button-impaired person who claims that the fax machine and the copier are mysteries and who is constantly jamming their paper feeds does not, you will notice, ever have to send faxes or make copies. Don't give this person a "pass go" card. Ask the most patient person in the office to demystify the machines and the paper feeds for your cleverly inept coworker.

When you aren't able to straightforwardly delegate a job, and you need to persuade someone to do it, the most effective way is to point out the ways in which what you want this person to do actually benefits them. Some people think that persuasion involves talking very fast and cleverly. On the contrary, it is better done by listening. Ask questions ("How would you do this?") and urge the person to talk about the task ("Tell me what you think").

Ask for Help

If you're open to suggestions, express your frustration with time to the people closest to you and ask if they have any insights into your busyness. They may not have been aware of your struggles. Now they can be more sensitive about asking for your time. They may see possibilities for small fine-tuning of your use of time. Or they may mention unthinking habits of yours that consume minutes and hours. At the very least, discussing this with someone who cares about you may produce some good brainstorming.

Spend Money Instead of Time

For most of us, this isn't always a possible solution. But at least do the math. If you are self-employed, know what your time is worth so that you can compute whether it makes financial sense for you to continue working at your desk for an hour for $35 while paying someone $15 an hour to mow the lawn or clean the house. Sometimes you're better off doing the yard or the house yourself because you can sandwich chores in between phone calls or computer sessions and not lose too much work time.

Get Enough Sleep

The classic example of spending time to save time is getting the amount of sleep that's right for you. A very superficial test to see if you're getting enough sleep is to try to go to sleep several times throughout the day. If you go unconscious every time you try this, you're probably not getting enough sleep. If you shut your eyes for five or ten minutes but don't fall asleep, you're probably getting enough.

Marketing and productivity consultant Gary Bencivenga (www.success bullets.com) says, "Research shows that your productivity, clarity, alertness, judgment, creativity, memory, motivation, relaxation, cheerfulness, and lots of other wonderful qualities all thrive on adequate sleep and suffer without it."

Waiting

Despite calling ahead and despite verifying an appointment, we often end up waiting for someone or something. Use that time. If you're a busy person, the best use of that time might be to completely relax your body and meditate—something as simple as breathing slowly in and out while clearing your mind of everything but a mantra ("thank you" is always good). This little habit will do you more good than squeezing in a few minutes of reading or making phone calls.

Or daydream. Shut your eyes and look at the big picture of your life. Imagine success; imagine happiness; place yourself mentally in a beautiful place.

If you're a different sort of person, carry some catch-up reading with you: reports, magazines, your current book, or even letters. Your waiting time will fly by, and you won't end up irritated and flustered.

Self-Talk

Sometimes your own expectations may cause you to shoot yourself in the foot. You might look at perfectionism, for example. In some areas of life, perfectionism may be something to aim for. We all would certainly like to find high levels of perfectionism on the job in our airline pilots, doctors and nurses, emergency technicians, and elected officials. Or, anyway, in our airline pilots, doctors and nurses, and emergency technicians. But does the airline pilot have to have a perfectly manicured yard? Does the doctor have to serve five-course dinners?

> *I think perfectionism is based on the obsessive belief that if you run carefully enough, hitting each stepping-stone just right, you won't have to die. The truth is that you will die anyway and that a lot of people who aren't even looking at their feet are going to do a whole lot better than you, and have a lot more fun while they're doing it.*
> —ANNE LAMOTT (1994)

Figure out where it will pay you, literally and figuratively, to aim for the best possible job you can do. And then do a "good enough" job the rest of the time.

Instead of talking to yourself as so many of us do ("Klutz," "Dummy," "You'll never get this done," "If only I had another couple of hours in the day"), seek out positive messages, and repeat them often to yourself:

- ▶ "You'll get it done."
- ▶ "You've always met your deadlines in the past."
- ▶ "There's enough time for everything you need to do."
- ▶ "You've done your best; now stop thinking about it."
- ▶ "Trust yourself on this one."
- ▶ "Good job."
- ▶ "Thanks, Self, for leaving me a clean desk to come back to."
- ▶ "Thanks, Self, for filing that contract just where I could find it." *
- ▶ "I always get the important things finished."

Small Time-Savers

▶ Keep postcards on hand, and send a postcard instead of a letter.

▶ Make your list for tomorrow this evening, preferably right after dinner, so that you can enjoy the rest of the evening, knowing that tomorrow is tomorrow and that, for now, the day is done. Otherwise you'll spend the evening thinking about what needs to be done tomorrow. An added benefit is that your brain can be playing with that list while you sleep, possibly developing additions, elaborations, and solutions.

▶ In the same way, draw up your To Do list for tomorrow before you leave work each day. You can then put work completely out of your mind and enjoy the evening ahead.

▶ If clothes need to be drycleaned or laundered, do it right after you've worn them.

▶ When you're traveling, do your packing the night before, with clothes to go in at the last minute and your morning-use things set aside. Otherwise you won't sleep as well, as you'll wake periodically to remind yourself not to forget this or that. For a family trip, pack the car with as much as you can the night before. In the morning confusion, you'll be glad you did.

▶ When you consistently run over deadlines, take a look at how you're estimating projects. You may be unrealistic about how much you can accomplish within set time limits. Look at past projects' actual completion times to set new deadlines.

▶ When employees or coworkers are late for an appointment or meeting with you—depending on the frequency and severity of their unpunctuality—you might say something like, "We're going to have to do this some other time. It's really too late to get much done in the time I have left." If your supervisors or bosses are habitually late, there's not much you can do except check with their assistants beforehand to see if they're running on schedule.

▶ If you come across something that will take only a couple of minutes or less to finish or put where it belongs, do it now. Yesterday's paper?

Recycle it now. A burnt-out lightbulb? Replace it now. The grand-father clock has stopped? Wind it now. A report that needs routing? Slap a sticky note on it and put it in your outbox now. If you did all these things at once, it would take a chunk of time. But if you go about your day spending one minute here and two minutes there on small actions, it takes virtually no time, yet you're keeping the machinery that you depend on in motion.

▶ Buffer appointments and activities scheduled on your calendar with enough time between them so that in the interval you can respond to an emergency, assemble your thoughts, repack your briefcase, and, above all, not feel hurried and harried. You'll feel more in control of your life if you can go from appointment to appointment in a col-lected fashion.

▶ Even if you do nothing but shove everything together in piles, try to leave your desk in good shape for the next day. There's nothing more dispiriting than coming in, finding a mess, and wondering where to start. You're doing this for *you*. Be nice to yourself. Some mornings you'll want to give yourself a big hug for leaving things so nice for you.

▶ Keep spare working pens and notepads not only on your desk, but in your briefcase, purse, glove compartment, and pocket, and near every phone in your life.

▶ Some theorists think that one reason we feel overwhelmed is the abundance of choices available to us. Minimizing choices in your life can free you from some pedestrian business. For example, if you're in the market for white socks, you have to choose among men's, women's, acrylic, cotton, cotton blend, terry, orlon, wool, polyamide, Lycra spandex, elastic, athletic, leisure, low-cut, footie, ankle-length, crew, over-the-calf, over-the-knee, lightweight, ultra-lite, no-show, quarter-height, thigh-high, ribbed, slouch, and cushioned foot. So if you find socks that you like, buy the same brand and size and type all the time, ordering them online in bulk. Once you become aware of the complexity of choice in the United States, you can understand why some of us are too busy. The decision-making part of our brain, which we badly need for work and for survival, is being used up on, yes, socks. If standardizing some of your choices makes you feel uncreative, you can still be adventurous with your choice of airlines-without-services and restaurants-without-numbers. Some people have standing orders for some office and home supplies. It's not a bad idea.

▶ Anything you do over and over again should be systematized. Reinventing the wheel is a waste of time. If you write monthly reports, you no doubt always use the same form or format. Carry this over to all the jobs that you have to repeat.

▶ Keep in mind that saving time is not an end in itself. Try not to become obsessed with minutes and hours. You want to give a task all the time it needs—but no more. Use the time you save gratefully and gracefully. You will not feel so harried if you can remember a leisure hour that you spent the way you wanted to spend it.

Part Three

Getting Organized Everywhere

CHAPTER 7

How to Organize Your Office

It is curious how any making of order makes
one feel mentally ordered, ordered inside.

—MAY SARTON (1954)

You spend most of your waking hours in your office. Ideally, it
should be pleasant, practical, and efficient—helping you to do
your best work, rather than hindering you from doing so.

The most important decision you make—if you get to make this one—
is the shape of your work area. All other things being equal, a U-shaped
workspace is probably the most sensible. You can, of course, buy lovely
office furniture in the U shape, but you can also create your own using a
basic office desk, a computer desk, a bridge or connector or return, and a
set of bookshelves. You can do the same thing with an L-shaped desk,
a bridge/connector/return piece, and bookshelves. The shelves take the
burden off your desk as far as books, paper trays, accessories, and other
accoutrements go.

If you haven't got a window and will be looking at a wall anyway, consider a space-saving corner desk or L-shaped desk using a corner.

If you don't much like visitors, arrange your desk so that your back is
to the door.

When you're given an office or a cubicle or a desk, it doesn't have to stay
in its original state. Think about how you work, and take a little time in the
beginning to arrange things to your satisfaction.

Partition Your Office

You don't need to physically partition your office, unless, of course, that's possible. But mentally divide your office into dedicated work zones. This is, once more, a case of grouping like functions or like activities. The more you can think of your office as being composed of zones, according to function, the more efficient you'll be. For example:

▶ *Work area.* The top of your desk and perhaps part of a computer return is your main work area. It needs to be kept as clear as possible. Give it a good look to make sure there's nothing here that belongs somewhere else. This is where you keep a few items that you reach for constantly. For some people, this is a cellophane tape dispenser; for others it's paperclips, or a stapler, or scissors. A clock, desk lamp, or your business cards in a holder might be here. Most of us keep a pen holder because we're always reaching for a pen or marker or highlighter. Also helpful in this area is a set of wooden or plastic in/out trays. Label each tray so that you don't confuse your To File tray with your To Sort tray.

▶ *Computer area.* Depending on your equipment, keep your CPU, monitor, keyboard, mouse, printer/copier/fax/scanner, speakers, external drives, power backup, and all items that you sometimes hook up (camera, travel drive) as close together as possible. If space is at a premium, set your printer on one of the specially made add-on shelves so that you can keep printer paper and cartridges underneath.

> Order is ... the true key to rapidity of reaction.
> —Maria Montessori (1917)

▶ *Telephone area.* A pad of scratch paper and a pencil are all you need near the phone. However, one of the most important items in your entire office is your address book. For all of us today, our list of family, friends, and business contacts is more important than ever. It needs to be complete and accessible. There are several ways to do this, along with ensuring that if you lose your main list, you'll have a backup list:

- A Rolodex keeps contact information on cards mounted on a rotating desktop holder. Although *rolodex* is often used as a generic term, Newell Rubbermaid's Rolodex (a combination of "rolling" and "index") is the prototype and probably still the best of its type. The advantage of the Rolodex is that it sits right by your phone and you can pull off outdated cards and insert new cards at will. Its main disadvantage is that you can't do a global search when you have only a phone number (left in a message), only a first name that you can remember, or only a town that rings a bell. The chances of losing or misplacing your Rolodex are so infinitesimal that there is no backup plan suggested.

- An address book, in the old-fashioned sense of a notebook that you carry with you, is useful because of its portability, not so useful for the same reason as the Rolodex, and usually more trouble to keep current. It's also cumbersome to make a backup copy of it, either by manually reproducing it or by trying to photocopy its pages, and its very portability increases the chances of losing or misplacing it.

- Having all your names and addresses on your computer (using dedicated software or simply keeping linear lists) makes things easy in a number of ways: (1) you can add and delete easily without affecting the rest of your information, (2) you can do global searches or search fields to find people or ZIP codes or categories or area codes, (3) you can cut and paste when you need to put information in a document, (4) you can print out addresses by category, (5) you can transfer some or all of your address files to your BlackBerry or other electronic organizer, and vice versa, and (6) you can break down your addresses by the way in which you use them: family members and friends, work contacts, college alumni/ae, overseas, hometown, committee members, board members. Because this list is so central to your life, it must be backed up regularly in whatever way you back up your hard drive. If you keep a copy of the list on your handheld device, that will serve as a copy as long as you keep it updated. With a travel drive, you can copy the updated list onto your home computer or electronic device so that you have copies at home, at work, and with you.

▶ *Mail area.* In this area (probably on one side of your desk), you keep a letter opener; a wastebasket and a recycling bin (for magazines and newspapers); an out tray (or equivalent), so that some mail can be turned around immediately, ready to go in the next mail or be forwarded to a coworker; and an in tray (or equivalent) for mail that you still need to deal with. In a home office, this is where you'll keep your mailing materials: postal scale, postage stamps, and mailing labels.

▶ *Shelves area.* If you are the type who never saw an empty shelf that you couldn't fill, you might have to watch yourself with shelving, what with nature abhorring a vacuum and all that. But shelves can be the making of an office. Think creatively and install shelves wherever you have dead space. Keep necessary books there, as well as accordion files for ongoing projects, equipment that you don't use often (paper hole punch, for example), and office supplies. If you use see-through bins or boxes, you'll save time finding things. Alternatively, if the bins or boxes you use aren't see-through, be sure to label them. You can use double-sided shelves for a room divider, or low shelves with a spacious top to provide you with a working area or a place for your printer and its supplies.

▶ *Outgoing area.* Whether you are leaving your desk, your cubicle, your office, or your home, this area is near the door. One spot holds everything you might need to take with you when you leave your office: work materials that belong to someone else; your briefcase; a carryall to hold smaller items that go with you; gifts or drycleaning or other items to be delivered; and your jacket or coat, scarf, umbrella, or outerwear. In certain cases, your keys go on a hook by the door.

▶ *Reception area.* If you have business visitors, you might have several chairs, a coffee table or end table, and a coat tree in one corner.

▶ *Reading area.* An upholstered chair, a good reading lamp, and a table surface allow you to leave your desk for periods of reading. One woman calls it her thinking chair. When she's finished thinking, she moves to the working chair at her desk. This is probably a luxury for most people, but it doesn't hurt to dream. Keep all books in this area except for any reference books that you use several times a day (they'll go in your work area).

▶ *Specialty area.* Your work may involve mock-ups or models, piles of samples, drawing materials, swatches of material, or other items. Keep these separate from your work area.

Basic Office Supplies

Not everyone will need all the things that are listed here, especially since galloping technology means that some of us still have mouse pads and some of us don't, but it makes a good checklist and indicates how you might group the items:

Paper Supplies

Laser or ink-jet paper

Copier paper

Letterhead stationery

Second sheets of letterhead (plain)

Scrap paper for notes

Sticky-backed notes

Notecards for thank-you and congratulations messages

Postcards

#10 letterhead envelopes

#9 envelopes if you often enclose a SASE

9×12″ manila envelopes

10×13″ manila envelopes

Bubble envelopes of various sizes

Labels: return address, shipping, file, and disk

File folders

Cardboard mailers

3×5″ and 4×6″ index cards

Notebooks, spiral or pad

Business cards

Equipment

Desktop computer

Printer/copier/fax/scanner and refill cartridges

Telephone and headset

Calculator (if you don't use your computer for it)

Computer-Related

Storage disks

Batteries

Screen cleaner

Mouse pad

Writing Materials

Pens

Highlighters

Pencils

Marking pens

Pencil sharpener

Reference Works

Dictionary

Thesaurus

Work-related references

Computer and software manuals

Office Aids

Business card holder

Cellophane tape and dispenser

Clipboard

Clock

Correction fluid

Desk lamp

Hole punch

Label maker

Letter opener

Paperclips, binder clips, brads

Recycling bins

Rubber bands

Rubber stamps and ink pads

Ruler

Scissors

Stapler, staples, and staple remover

Trays (in, out, and other)

Wastebasket

Tips

▶ Use your walls. Shelves can be installed 6 to 12 inches under the ceiling, allowing their tops to also serve as storage for items you need but don't use very often. Install vertical paper files (angled pockets) to keep stacks of enclosures, brochures, office forms, or other papers that you want to have available but not taking up space on or in your desk. (You can add additional pockets as needed.) A three-tiered wire basket on a wall or ceiling hanger can hold rolls of tape or other small supplies where they can be readily seen but are taking up space that otherwise wouldn't be used.

▶ Use boilerplates or macros as much as you can. Any text that you use over and over without changing it can be turned into a macro. Then you need to strike only one or two keys for the macro to appear where your cursor is. Voilà! Just where you want it is:

- Your name and address

- Your e-mail address

- A paragraph thanking the writer for writing

- Your sign-off and signature

- Several paragraphs rejecting a submission

- Several paragraphs rejecting a submission but suggesting that the person contact you with other material

In short, any sentence, phrase, paragraph, or letter that you use often can be turned into a macro.

▶ If you have a corded phone (something that's still handy when the electricity goes out), put a 25- or 50-foot cord on it. If space is at a premium and you prefer keeping your desk surface as free as possible for work, consider a wall phone placed where you can reach it from your desk chair.

▶ Sticky-back notes are useful, but they are easily detached and lost, so use them only on items that won't be shuffled about.

▶ If you must sign your name many times a day, consider an electronic or digitized signature, which looks just as though you had signed the letter yourself. (Check the possible legal implications of using such a signature on contracts or other binding documents.)

▶ If you spend a lot of time at conferences or on the road, you could probably paper your office with the business cards people have handed you. Holders and albums are designed to keep these cards, but you're much better off inputting the data for any person you want to keep track of in a computer file. It's much easier to do a global search of a file for a certain name or product or company than to thumb through dozens of cards—or to give them shelf space in your office. Better yet, get a business-card reader that will scan the cards. Software allows you to organize and access these cards by various fields.

▶ A bulletin board (or cork squares arranged like one) always *seems* like a good idea, but in actual practice, it's not too useful in an office. Either it becomes a dumping ground for things you haven't looked at in months or you lose interest and it's one more messy thing to think about. However, there are people (not many, admittedly) who make excellent use of them. Just make sure you're one of these people before buying one.

▶ Dedicate each desk drawer to a specific purpose. One can be for "tools": scissors, stapler, tape, correction fluid, glue, extra pens, pen cartridges, coins for parking or snack machines, and so on. One might be dedicated to mailing supplies—enough letterhead envelopes to take care of you for a month, postage stamps, labels, or rubber stamps if you use them. To organize your desk, remove everything—everything!—and lay it out on the floor or on your desktop. Sort by like items—all the pencils together, and so on. When you have everything in piles (you might also have a ? pile), decide which items you use the least. They go in a bottom drawer. Which do you use most often? They belong in a top drawer. After you've put things in drawers, you might see a use for a divider or for small clear boxes to keep things separate. When you're finished, keep all your desk drawers pulled out, and study them for a few minutes. Is this the way you work? Will you remember where things go? If not, you might need to rearrange things most conveniently for yourself.

▶ One attractive upright container on your desktop can hold the items you use most often: letter opener, pens, pencils, scissors, magnifying glass. Keep extra pens and pencils with your supplies.

▶ If you're always charging your electronics, put all the cords, plugged into a power strip, in one out-of-the-way place. You can even Velcro the power strip to the wall at the back of a bookcase or cabinet. To handle and hide the many cables you may have in your office, study some of the numerous solutions and gadgets found online. You shouldn't have to look at, or trip on, your power supplies.

▶ Your office can appear more streamlined if you use the same one or two colors throughout, buy shelving and matching storage bins that look inconspicuous, and keep as many surfaces clear as you can. If you crave color, choose one fun piece for your wall, desk, or tabletop.

▶ Keep your briefcase either by the door, so that you don't forget it (and whenever you have something going home with you, put it in there immediately), or under your desk, so that you can drop items into it that you'll need for a meeting, an appointment, or taking home. Stock your briefcase once with items that you almost always need (business cards, pens, notepads, a clipboard, tissues, a spare set of keys), and replace them as needed. Then you need only remember to add whatever current papers are necessary and your BlackBerry or cell phone.

Organizing Aids

▶ *Calendar.* Depending how you work, you'll want to use a software calendar on your computer, a big wall calendar that you can read from your desk, or a daily desk calendar with perhaps some nice artwork on the facing pages. What's most useful is your list of dates (see Chapter 3). No matter how else you keep track of events and appointments and other activities, everything needs to go on that list so that you can make connections among the different parts of your life and see at a glance everything that's coming up without having to click a mouse or turn pages.

▶ *Filing cabinets.* Not everyone today needs the filing cabinets that once were standard equipment. It's entirely possible to get by with several accordion files for current projects arranged on a bookshelf. Once the project is completed, the file is sorted for unnecessary papers, tied up, labeled, and stored. If you have a file drawer in your desk, it might take care of all your files.

▶ *Multifunction equipment.* The obvious example is the single machine that prints, faxes, copies, and scans. Your phone also serves several purposes. It should contain your most-often-used telephone numbers, saving you the lookup time; you can leave yourself messages on it, using the memo function; you can have several voice mailboxes for different aspects of your job, if that's effective for you; cordless phones allow you to walk about the building. You can use a rolling cart to store items, to bring next to your desk when you need an extra surface to work on, and to move heavy boxes around.

- *Multipurpose furniture.* Use double-sided open shelving that can be accessed from both sides while serving as a room divider; instead of a sleek, slab-type modern desk, choose one with file drawers or shelves, or use file cabinets with a wood slab on top that provides work space; choose a wooden chair that converts to a stepladder for reaching high shelves.

- *Storage units.* Stacking boxes, bins, wicker baskets, and trays come in many colors and sizes. Restrained and effective use of them can clear your office of paperwork and supplies while allowing you to find what you need when you need it.

- *Shelving and bookcases.* Odd-shaped offices benefit from built-in shelving that uses narrow, otherwise dead space.

The Home Office

The home office has two special challenges: (1) dealing with people is more difficult, as others are less likely to understand that you are "at work" when you are "at home" (see Chapter 5 for help with this), and (2) carving out an adequate and private space can be a problem, especially if you live with others. Everything said in this chapter about the ideal office holds true for home offices. But life being less than ideal, you may have to settle for what you can assemble. The basics for a home office include (1) a door between you and the rest of the house that can be shut, (2) a telephone, (3) a work surface, (4) a desk chair, (5) file cabinets and/or shelves, (6) a desktop computer and a printer/copier/fax/scanner, and (7) space for supplies.

Before you spend a great deal of money setting yourself up in a home office, you need to be fairly certain that it's going to work for you. Some people are, this very minute, going stir-crazy in lovely home offices. If at all possible, give yourself three to six months of working at home before you invest in your dream office.

If you must work at home, factor in your issues with being alone eight hours a day. Perhaps you can spend an hour or two a day at a café (but be careful of working on files with sensitive data when you're using public wireless setups). Or consider sharing a home office—theirs or yours—with someone like you.

Tips

▶ You must have at least a two-line phone (three if you live with others). One line should be free for incoming calls while you use the second line for outgoing calls.

▶ When your space is limited, consider pull-down shelves or a pull-down table for use when you're compiling materials or otherwise temporarily need extra space. Storage boxes or bins are stackable, and you can put a lot of paperwork (if you really need to keep it) in a few square feet. The vertical files mentioned earlier are especially good in a home office because they require so little space. Inexpensive stacking drawers come in wood, acrylic, and cardboard. They aren't as sturdy as some storage solutions, but they don't take up much space, and with the acrylic ones, you can see at a glance what's in them.

▶ If you have a window in your home office, consider blinds because in many cases, you'll want to alter the slant of the sun at certain times of day, depending on the room's location.

CHAPTER 8

How to Organize Your Home Space

*In violent and chaotic times such as these, our
only chance for survival lies in creating our own
little islands of sanity and order, in making little
havens of our homes.*

—SUE KAUFMAN (1974)

I f possible, zone your home by function: all food preparation and
eating take place in one continuous area, which might include kitchen,
pantry, breakfast nook or bar counter, and dining room; sleeping and
quiet areas are separated from noisy areas by halls, staircases, or other
natural buffers; common areas like living room and recreation room or
den and outdoor patio or deck would constitute a third broad zone. This
isn't always possible, but a home—whether it's an apartment or a three-
story mansion—needs to provide areas principally for sleep, for eating,
and for enjoying leisure, and it's easier to do this and keep a home organized if they are separated from one another.

If you're starting fresh, or even doing over, think of an adjective for your
home. Will someone walk in and exclaim, "My, what a *friendly* home"? Or
will the adjective be *elegant* or *homey* or *cheerful* or *happy* or *sophisticated*?
Obviously no one wants that adjective to be *messy* or *disorderly* because no
one ever specifically plans to have that sort of home. By focusing on what
you do want your home to be, you can work toward that image of it, and
you will be more motivated to keep it the way you have envisioned it.

Living Areas

The living areas of your home can include a living room, a recreation room, a den, a family room, or even a study. Anywhere that you are not eating or sleeping, you are assumed to be living.

Whether you live alone or with others, determine your needs for this part of the house. The minimum is probably a sofa, a coffee table, a chair, and a floor lamp. You can trade the coffee table for an end table, in which case the floor lamp becomes a table lamp. Adding on gets you flooring, more chairs, and a television. From there you can go on to wall art and more tables and lamps—in fact, space and money are the only limits.

Consider: Is this particular room reserved for visitors? Is it used only by family members? Is it a destination for one person, who comes there to go unconscious on the couch? Spend time imagining before you start painting or buying furniture. Picture the way the room is used, and make a list of items that will support those activities.

If more than one person uses the room, consider multiple-use zoning: a television viewing corner, a reading nook, a games table, and a piano-playing area.

You can save yourself a great deal of upkeep by buying items that can't easily be injured (marble tabletops), that don't stain (treated materials), that don't show dirt (darker or multicolored fabrics), that have drawers in which oddments can be stashed, or that are on casters so that they can be moved easily for cleaning. Think ahead. Every good decision now means less work for you in the future.

Tips

► Whenever you have a choice, buy multifunction furniture: sofa beds; futons; ottomans with a lid and storage space inside; a "sleeper ottoman" that opens into a bed; benches that double as storage chests; trunks or hope chests that double as benches with a cushion on top or as low tables with a tray on top; serving carts, tea tables, and coffee tables with removable trays and storage underneath; kitchen butcher blocks on wheels (that can be locked when in place) that can extend a counter, be moved closer to the stove, or stay in the middle of the kitchen; wine racks that also hold wineglasses; nested tables; high-quality (wooden, leather-topped ones are nice) folding TV trays that can be used as end tables; or dual-sided bookshelves that can serve as room dividers.

▶ We are generally so visual that we choose furniture on the basis of its shape, color, and texture and how well it fits with everything else. Don't forget comfort. If you ever have to sit through an evening watching a guest try to get comfortable in one of your chairs, you will test-drive every piece of furniture before arranging for delivery.

> *I love it—I love it; and who shall dare*
> *To chide me for loving that old arm-chair?*
> —ELIZA COOK (1848)

▶ Nobody really likes them, but if you have small children and lovely new furniture, invest in clear plastic protective covers for the next few years.

▶ Look at space creatively. A swiveling CD tower can store twice as much in half the space. Shelving for little-used books or collections can run around the entire room at ceiling level, using otherwise dead space. Wall-hung shelving and shallow cabinets can fill empty spaces while providing storage. Corner cabinets, corner wine racks, and corner shelving can take advantage of a little wall space to bring you a lot of storage. Armless sofas can seat more people.

> *It's just as possible to live to the full in a narrow corner as it is in bigness.*
> —SYLVIA ASHTON-WARNER (1963)

▶ Keep all remotes in a dedicated remote organizer or in a straw basket and request that they always be returned to their place.

► Unsightly but useful cables and cords have multiplied in our homes. When possible, group all electronic devices in one area of the room. Plug all cords and charging cables into a surge protector power strip and bundle the cords in a cable cover or raceway. Worst-case scenario: attach the cords to the wall (being very careful not to puncture them) and paint them the same color as the wall. You can sometimes mount a power strip on the wall if that helps or look for a swivel outlet surge protector—the outlets can swivel to better accommodate your cords.

> *Life is a verb, not a noun.*
> —CHARLOTTE PERKINS
> GILMAN (1904)

► Because life is a verb, our living areas tend to get more disorganized more quickly than any room except the kitchen. Newspapers, books, magazines, mail, shoes, sweaters, dog collars, and other odds and ends litter every surface. The rule is fairly simple: before leaving the room, take with you everything you brought in or put back everything you took out (remote, magazine, footstool).

► When cleaning your living areas, don't forget to wash light fixtures, clean vents, replace air filters, dust or wash ceiling fans, and wipe down the walls. Vacuum under furniture and remove all furniture cushions to vacuum underneath them; flip cushions to lessen wear on one side only.

► Add a good-quality extension cord to your vacuum cleaner. And if you have high ceilings or ceiling fans, invest in a long-handled pole with cleaning attachments.

Kitchen

Zoning and grouping are especially useful in the kitchen. In an ideal world, you would zone the kitchen according to (1) food storage, (2) food preparation, (3) serveware (bowls, tableware, silverware, and glassware), and (4) cleanup. In the real world, do the best you can to keep these four kitchen functions separate.

Within those areas, group like items. If you have a little time on your hands and want some fun (and your kitchen is extremely disorganized), pull out everything from your kitchen shelves and put it on the floor. From there, do the traditional sorting:

▶ Toss

▶ Give-away

▶ Return to its place

▶ ?

When returning items to cupboards and shelves, place them nearest where you will be using them in groups of similar items:

> *I don't like to say that my kitchen is a religious place, but I would say that if I were a voodoo princess I would conduct my rituals there.*
> —PEARL BAILEY (1999)

▶ Plates, glasses, bowls, mugs

▶ Baking pans, muffin tins, cookie sheets

▶ Preparation items—bowls, mixers, measuring cups

▶ Cooking items—pots, skillets, Dutch ovens, double boilers

▶ Canned and boxed goods

▶ Baking and cooking goods—flour, sugar, herbs, spices, oils

▶ Dry goods—tablecloths, dishtowels, aprons

▶ Cleaning products

Tips

▶ If space is limited, choose smaller-than-standard, space-saving appliances (refrigerators, stoves, dishwashers, wine coolers). Especially if you live alone, these are usually more than adequate. Some stores specialize in this type of appliance, including washer-dryer combos and sinks. In the same way, look for open cabinets or frameless kitchen cabinets, which take up a little less space and offer a little more storage, and run the cabinets all the way to the ceiling. To achieve an illusion of spaciousness in a small kitchen, limit colors to one or two, choose cabinets of a uniform style and color, and keep the counters cleared.

▶ One bit of wasted space that few of us notice is found in cupboards where plates, cans, or glasses use only half the height of the cupboard. You can install another shelf partway up. This isn't always a good idea (think of trying to extract something from the back), but if you have tall cupboards, you might check for unused vertical space. Alternatively, add handy multilevel storage units (rubber- or plastic-coated steel wire) to take advantage of the available space.

▶ Another bit of useful space is that between counters and the underside of cupboards. While you don't want to overdo it, a few things can be attached to the cupboard bottoms: a paper towel holder doesn't take up much space; some can openers will go there nicely; you can even screw in hooks and hang coffee mugs there.

▶ Small appliances can overwhelm the largest countertops. If you use an appliance daily (coffeemaker, toaster, electric kettle, or can opener), it can stay out, but everything else should find cupboard space. It's better to have to take out the breadmaker or blender once a week than to lose valuable counter space to it. Sliding pullout shelves are especially handy for storing small appliances.

▶ If you need extra workspace, install a flip-up counter at the end or even a long one on the side of an existing counter. Butcher blocks and tables that fold up or that are mounted on casters are useful and adaptable.

▶ Few kitchens have all the shelf and cupboard space that they need. Give your kitchen a careful look for areas where you could hang shelves—over a door, up under the ceiling, between appliances, or on top of low-hung cabinets. You can find, for example, very narrow sliding units that can be pulled out from between, say, the stove and the refrigerator. It's enough space to store all your canned goods. If you can conceive of a storage solution, you can probably find it online somewhere.

She was a natural-born cook ... People gnawed their fingers and bit their tongues just to smell the steam when she lifted the pot lids.

—JULIA PETERKIN (1927)

- If lighting is poor, you can upgrade to a better overhead light, but it may still be difficult for you to see what you're doing on a counter when you stand between the ceiling light and the counter. Inexpensive under-cabinet lighting is very simple to install and will illuminate your work area.

- The kitchen is a good place to keep a small toolbox of repair items: a hammer, a Phillips and a flat screwdriver, pliers, heavy-duty strapping or electrical tape, a paintbrush, a putty knife, glues, and a handful of various size nails.

- Most kitchens need a temporary place for papers and phone messages. If a kitchen desk is not your main paperwork site (see the section "The Home Office" in Chapter 9), keep a tray to catch flying papers, but transfer them to that main paperwork site at least once a day. One area of the kitchen is often a message center with telephone, paper-catching tray, calendar, and dry-erase board (see the section "Organizing Your Family" in Chapter 9).

- When you replace the full kitchen garbage bag in its container, put a handful of bags under the clean one. That way, you've got one ready to go the next time.

- Get into the habit of cleaning out the refrigerator (and emptying all baskets in the house) the night your trash goes out. Then when you make up your shopping list, you won't mistake your shriveled red peppers for tomatoes and that green stuff for fresh arugula. Not only will you be able to see better, but putting your groceries away when you get back from the store will be much more pleasant.

- Depending on your taste, you might consider open shelving so that you can see where everything is. This convention is a great inspiration for keeping things neat. And if you use, for example, only bright yellow dishes, bowls, mugs, and pitchers, it is

Kitchens were different then, too—not only what came out of them, but their smells and sounds. A hot pie cooling smells different from a frozen pie thawing.
—PEG BRACKEN (1981)

attractive as well. The big inconvenience with open shelving is dust and debris. Glass doors solve this, but they come with their own issue: fingerprints. If this is your style, you'll also like clear containers that show you how much sugar or coffee or spaghetti is left.

► Organized shopping starts with meal planning. Draw up a list of groceries based on what you expect to be eating in the next week or two. It helps to have a standardized list (see Chapter 3) of the foods that you buy most often. You can then leave these items on the list or delete those that you don't currently need. Shop strictly to your list; being in a hurry helps you stay honest. Not being hungry is another good help. It's probably worth the price of a banana split, eaten before you enter the grocery store, in terms of what you'll save in impulse buying. All food will look disgusting to you at that point, but, list in hand, you'll reluctantly buy the items you need. Impulse buying is the biggest cause of bigger grocery bills and wasted food (you might eat the impulsive purchase, but the leaf spinach on your list probably will not get eaten). Coupons may not be in your best budget interests. Few manufacturers offer coupons on things that you regularly need and use. Stay with your list, with generics, and with the more healthful fresh foods and produce (which seldom come with coupons). And remember to bring your own canvas bags or insulated market bags to save on "paper or plastic."

► Many people find that they save time and money by buying in bulk and vacuum-sealing for the freezer. You almost have to try this to discover whether it works for you or whether food ages and dies in your freezer before you remember to use it.

The interest in good meals is universal.
—LOUISE M. NEUSCHUTZ
(1948)

► One way to save money on food is simply to avoid wasting any. Apparently some 12 percent of the landfill in the United States consists of uneaten food; one report says that as much as 30 percent of U.S. food is wasted annually. This global problem filters right down to your house: a U.S. family of four wastes at least $600 worth of food per year. The most important way to cut down on waste is to wrap leftovers properly and then use them the next day—disguised, if you think that will help. Don't overbuy, and always shop with a list. Make a mental note of what you most often end up throwing out and resolve either not to buy it again or to buy or prepare less of it. Having plastic baggies, aluminum and plastic wrap, and lidded plastic containers on hand will make it much easier for you to keep food fresh and edible.

▶ If you clean one area of the kitchen each week or even each month, you can cycle through the year without having to take everything apart for a major cleaning.

- Refrigerator: remove food that is never going to be eaten; wipe down the shelves, walls, and bins with a dilute mixture of water and either baking soda or vinegar; rearrange items neatly; add an open box of baking soda to eliminate odors; unplug the refrigerator and vacuum beneath it, along the bottom, and behind it, if you can get there.

- Oven: remove racks; soak them in soapy water; scrape off baked-on material; brush out loose debris from the bottom; clean either with oven cleaner or with your automatic self-cleaning function; return clean racks.

- Dishwasher: remove racks and soak them in sudsy water; wipe the interior with water and vinegar or baking soda; run an empty load to rinse (and add any sponges that could use refreshing).

- Cupboards: empty, wash inside and out, restock items in an orderly way, while keeping an eye out for items that you haven't used since the last time you cleaned this cupboard. Those go in your Give-Away pile.

- Sink: the variety of materials used for sinks (stainless steel, cast iron, porcelain, quartz silicate, fireclay, vitreous china, natural stone) means that you can't use just any product on yours. Find out exactly what it's made of and what should be used to keep it looking good. Then go buy that product and never run out of it.

- Floors: again, your floor material (wood, stone, vinyl, or ceramic) will dictate how you clean them. Check once or twice a year for anything that may be degrading—missing grout, wood damage, chips, or holes. Much as you may dislike tending to these, doing so will help you escape major renovations in the future.

▶ If, for some odd reason, you could buy only one cleaning item for the kitchen, check out the BadBoy Cloth. It can be used for almost everything and is astonishingly effective.

▶ If you feel that your kitchen looks tired (remembering that it could be you who's tired), you can spiff it up simply and inexpensively by choosing new cupboard hardware. You'll feel like a child in a toyshop looking at the hundreds of different kinds of knobs and pulls and handles.

The dinner table is the center for the teaching and practicing not just of table manners but of conversation, consideration, tolerance, family feeling, and just about all the other accomplishments of polite society except the minuet.
—JUDITH MARTIN (1989)

▶ A three-tiered wire basket can be hung from the ceiling in a corner and filled with fresh fruit. The high visibility of the fruit seems to attract munchers, while the circulating air keeps the fruit fresher. You can also see instantly if a piece of fruit is bruised or rotting. The biggest advantage, though, is that it preserves counter space for cooking.

Friendships, like geraniums, bloom in kitchens.
—BLANCHE GELFANT (1985)

▶ When possible, triple recipes and freeze two batches. Whether it's cookies or casseroles, someday you'll think of yourself as your own best friend for having done so, and with some planning ahead (having enough ingredients), it doesn't take that much more time.

▶ Keep condiments or breakfast items (jams, butter, cream pitcher) on revolving trays in the refrigerator. It's easy to turn the tray to reach an item, and it's also easy to bring the entire tray to the table. Revolving trays are also handy in low, deep cupboards where it's difficult to see or reach items. We may

Eating without conversation is only stoking.
—Marcelene Cox (1943)

eventually see in this country the revolving tray table, where the elevated, revolving tray is a fixed part of the table, allowing all foods and condiments to be rotated to diners.

▶ If you get into the habit of putting spoons in one bin in the dishwasher, knives in another, and forks in another, you can return them to the silverware drawer afterward without having to sort them.

▶ Basic cleaning products that are usually kept in the kitchen (many of which come in environmentally friendly versions) include dishsoap and dishwasher detergent, scrubbing pads, sink cleaner (depending on what sink material you have), disposal cleaner, all-purpose cleaner, window cleaner, spot remover, sweeper (broom and dustpan, electric broom, or dust mop, depending on your floor type), mop, and bucket. Keep a basket near these and fill it with your specific cleaning needs when you are working in other rooms.

▶ In a household with children, any hazardous chemicals in the kitchen need to be in a locked cabinet.

There's no end to imagination in the kitchen.
—Julia Child (1986)

▶ A rag drawer or ragbag can save you up to $50 a year in paper towels as well as provide an end destination for linens, socks, underwear, and shirts that have reached the end of the line. Some spills (paint, eggs) call for a paper towel, but the average kitchen spill likes a cloth rag, which can then be washed.

Organizing Aids

▶ Hanging wire baskets
▶ Revolving trays

- ▶ Wine rack
- ▶ Folding or rolling butcher blocks and tables
- ▶ Drawer dividers
- ▶ Hooks
- ▶ Racks
- ▶ Trays
- ▶ Pull-out shelves
- ▶ Step stool or arm extender

Dining Room

When does the mind put forth its powers? when are the stores of memory unlocked? when does wit "flash from fluent lips?"—when but after a good dinner? Who will deny its influence on the affections? Half our friends are born of turbots and truffles.

—L. E. LANDON (1831)

The dining room doesn't seem to be as prominent as it once was. People entertain at home less often—and more casually when they do. However, those who have a dining room and its accoutrements—and who use it often—know what a joy it is to gather friends around a table for nourishment and conversation.

Some of what has been outlined in the section on the kitchen can be used for the dining room as well.

Tips

- ▶ Protect good china by putting paper plates or, a little more elegantly, tissue paper between them. China cups can also be separated by tissue paper or, less elegantly, coffee filters. However, unless you have troops of small children playing with water balloons in your dining room, you will do well if you simply and carefully arrange your china, wine and water glasses, and serving pieces in a china cabinet whose doors shut securely.

► A buffet or tea cart is handy as a side piece in the dining room, especially if it has a lower shelf or tray, and it can be wheeled into the living area for aperitifs before dinner or for after-dinner coffee.

► Since the dining room is fairly simple (table, chairs, and china cabinet and/or buffet), it doesn't need a lot of organizing. This is therefore a good room for your wild side: invite improbable people to dinner, use mismatched (but interesting) china, serve dishes that you've never tried before, tell jokes, and leave the room in disarray. Don't even clean it up until the next day. A little of this is a nice antidote to organizing everything else in the house.

Organizing Aids

► Buffet

► China cabinet

► Serving cart

► Silverware chest

► Wine rack

Bedrooms

The well-organized bedroom is both welcoming and functional. If you spend money anywhere, it probably ought to be on a bed that gives you a good night's sleep.

Beyond a bed, a dresser, and a closet, bedrooms don't need very much. You will add what you need in order to make the bedroom yours: reading lights, rugs if you have wood floors, other chests of drawers, and bedside tables.

The decor you choose—drapes or curtains, bedspread, flooring, rugs, and furniture—is of organizing interest only insofar as you choose items that are simple to keep up; for example, the bedspread and rugs can be washed instead of drycleaned, and the blinds serve as both curtains and shades, thus cutting down on upkeep.

Tips

▶ Children's bedrooms need extra planning to help the children keep their affairs in order. The more dedicated containers there are, the less likely it is that you will have to shovel out the room now and then. Have as much open shelving or storage cubes as the room will allow; it's true that shelves seem to invite

There is hardly any one in the civilized world—particularly of those who do just a little more every day than they really have strength to perform—who has not at some time regarded bed as a refuge.

—J. E. Buckrose (1923)

more items into the room, but that's better than having a littered floor. (If you fasten storage cubes to the walls instead of positioning them on the floor, be sure to attach them where there are studs.) Labeled boxes, bins, and baskets can hold toys—or shoes, socks, and T-shirts. Most children can be taught to use a hamper (with some instructions on what constitutes "needs to be washed"). Walls can be used to mount netting, tackboard, or canvas tool holders so that toys or display items have a special spot. Wall hooks or over-the-door hooks can hold jackets, schoolbags, sweaters, and baseball caps. Invite the room's occupant or occupants to help in the planning—especially in choosing wall colors, bedspreads, and ceiling (galaxies) or wall decorations. If you have several children, encourage them—if possible—to have wildly different decors; it's confidence building.

▶ Closets: According to John de Graaf, "New homes today have three times the closet space of homes built in the 1950s. The average house size has grown by 50% even as families have gotten smaller." Yet even with more closet space, "In the last few years, as companies like California Closets and the Container Store have expanded rapidly, the quest for the well-ordered closet has grown from a simple home design trend into a national preoccupation" (Stephanie Rosenbloom, "Into the Closet," *New York Times,* June 1, 2006).

Helen Kuhl, editor-in-chief of *Closets* magazine, says that Americans spend about $3 billion a year on closet-organizing systems. And that doesn't even include accessories like plastic shoe bins or the services of professional organizers specializing in closets (some of the latter charge $450 an hour).

This information is included here to make you feel really good about what you are about to do—using your own wits and a few inexpensive items from Target. The plan:

My bed is my best friend ... I type in it, telephone in it, think in it, and stare at the wall from it. Some morning, a long time from now, I hope I will be found peacefully dead in it, lying in a narrow but cozy space between old manuscripts, lost books, empty teacups, misplaced nightgowns, and unsharpened pencils.

—Jane O'Reilly (1980)

- Take absolutely everything out of the closet.

- Clean the closet thoroughly (a coat of paint doesn't cost as much as it will return you in good cheer).

- Sort everything you took out of the closet (be very stern here) into the things that are begging to be thrown away, the items that want to go to someone who will actually wear them, and those that you really want to keep.

- Check all the items you're keeping to see if they need repairs, laundering, or other attention.

- This is the time to add shelves if you have a tall closet.

- Assess everything that's going back in the closet and sort it by similarities: ties together, skirts together, shoes, hats, purses, slacks, suits, evening wear, outerwear, and the seldom worn.

- Decide what goes where in the closet.

- Identify organizers that will help you keep items tidy: a lower hanging rod for shirts or blouses, tie holders, hatboxes, shoe racks, slacks hangers, padded hangers, skirt hangers, wooden suit hangers, perhaps sturdy plastic hangers to replace the old wire ones that always get tangled up, multiple hangers (they have only one hook but can hold up to six hangered garments), over-the-door hangers and other organizers that can be attached to the inside of the closet door, shelves for the dead space high up in the closet.

- Return as much as you can to the closet, order or buy your organizers, and finish up.

- Take your extra wire hangers to the drycleaner next time you go.

- Be very proud.

▶ Once drawers get overstuffed, they're impossible to keep tidy, and you can find things only by pulling out items until you strike gold. Keep them about three-quarters full, with a little space to separate stacks or piles.

> *Keep things you use and create good karma by donating what you don't.*
> —ALYSON MCNUTT ENGLISH (2008)

▶ Hooks on the backs of doors or on walls keep robes, jackets, scarves, purses, and other items off the floor and off dresser tops. Hung low enough, they're especially good in children's rooms. Sometimes hanging up clothes takes more time than children want to spend, but a hook is conveniently quick.

▶ Beds can be raised on blocks made for that purpose to allow storage underneath. Drawers for storing out-of-season clothing or linens are made to fit under beds that aren't raised. Beds (usually intended for children) also come with built-in drawers. When space is tight, it's better to have storage under the bed than dust bunnies.

> *Most people spend their lives going to bed when they're not sleepy and getting up when they are!*
> —CINDY ADAMS (1957)

▶ Bedroom-cleaning checklist:

- Wash sheets and pillow slips.

- Wash blankets periodically.

- Wash or dryclean bedspreads and throw pillows periodically.

- Dust furniture.

- Vacuum or dust floor.

- Wash or dryclean rugs.

- Wash windows and blinds.

- Flip and rotate mattresses (flip Over in October, and switch Around in April).

- Sweep or dust under the bed.

- Check drawers to see that they are neat and that everything is where it belongs.

- Clear off the tops of nightstands, dressers, and desks as much as possible.

- Verify that the closet is clean and still organized.

- Check clothing and shoes for items that need cleaning or mending.

Organizing Aids

▶ Baskets, bins, and boxes

▶ Hamper

▶ Hanging organizers

▶ Jewelry chest

▶ Nonslip pants racks

▶ Over-the-door hooks

▶ Padded hangers

▶ Shelving

▶ Shoe racks

▶ Skirt and slacks hangers

▶ Storage cubes

▶ Tie racks

▶ Underbed storage drawers

Bathrooms

Bathrooms are tough. It's hard to zone what is often a small space, but if you can, separate—even artificially—the shower and/or tub area from the sink area from the toilet area.

In the shower area are bath towels and bath sheets; towel bars or hooks; the shower and/or tub; a holder for soaps, shampoo, bath gels, and scrubbers; and a bath mat.

In the sink area should be a flat area or counter, a cabinet to hold notions, a soap holder, toothbrush holders, hand towels, and towel bars.

The toilet area needs only a toilet tissue dispenser nearby. You can elaborate on these basics, depending on how much space you have.

Shelving or cabinetry to hold towels and backup bathroom supplies is especially useful in a bathroom. A variety of over-the-toilet cabinets are available. Few of them go to the ceiling, but you might want to think about using all the space you can for storage.

Tips

▶ We still call the mirrored cabinet that hangs over the bathroom sink a medicine cabinet. However, it properly should be used only for shaving equipment, notions and lotions, and other vanity items. Many medications don't do well in a humid environment, which the bathroom often is. Keep prescription medications in a cool, dry place that children cannot access. Keep a first-aid drawer or box in the linen closet, if you have one, or in the kitchen, high enough so that children can't reach it. Your first-aid basics include aspirin or ibuprofen, a variety of bandages, an antiseptic ointment, small scissors, tweezers, a thermometer, petroleum jelly, a Benadryl product, and sunscreen.

▶ If more than one adult lives in this house, the chore of cleaning the bathroom needs to be shared even-steven, for the simple reason that it makes everyone more careful about cleaning up after themselves.

- Remove and wash shower curtains.
- Clean shower walls, tub, and sink with an all-purpose cleaner or a mixture of water and vinegar or baking soda.
- Repair any missing caulking.
- Spray the entire outside of the toilet with disinfectant.
- Swab the inside of the toilet and bowl with a sponge brush.
- Wipe the outside of the toilet, starting from the top, being sure to do the back and around the bottom.
- Clean the mirror, light fixtures, and surfaces.
- Reorganize the medicine cabinet.
- Launder rugs.
- Scrub the floor.

▶ If you can keep from getting dirty and sweaty all over again, take a shower *before* you clean a bathroom. The steam will persuade dirt to come off walls, tiles, and porcelain more easily. You can also, while you're in the shower, wipe down the shower walls and door.

> *When I gave myself a home permanent and left it on too long, she was the only one to sit with me in the bathroom until it grew out.*
> —ERMA BOMBECK (1989)

▶ You probably can't have too many towel rods or hefty hooks in a bathroom, especially if more than one person uses it. If you don't have the wall space, but you do have extra floor space, try one of the standing coat racks with hooks up and down the pole; they keep towels smelling fresh because more of the towel is exposed to air, instead of touching itself on either side of a towel bar.

▶ A shower organizer that adjusts to the height of the shower ceiling (inside the pole are springs) and has several wire baskets extending from it is an incredibly useful invention. The wire or plastic organizer that hangs from the neck of the shower is not. You may also regret permanent fixtures to hold the soap, for example.

► Dr. Phillip Tierno, author of *The Secret Life of Germs*, says that you should rinse your toothbrush in mouthwash or peroxide before you use it. Every time the toilet is flushed, fecal bacteria are sprayed up to 20 feet into the air. If you keep your toothbrush in the bathroom, which most people do, at least house it in a drawer or the medicine cabinet so that you don't have to sanitize it every time. And always close the toilet lid before flushing.

► You can find corner toilets if you need to carve a bathroom out of a very small space, and they aren't that much more expensive than wall toilets.

Organizing Aids

► Hooks for robes

► Coat tree (makes an excellent hanger for wet towels)

► Towel bars

► Shelving

► Over-the-toilet cabinets

► "Medicine" cabinet

► Shower organizer

CHAPTER 9

How to Organize Your Home Life

*Each day, and the living of it, has to be a
conscious creation in which discipline and
order are relieved with some play and some
pure foolishness.*

—MAY SARTON (1973)

Now that your furnishings and possessions are in place and nicely organized, the wild rumpus begins. Life itself takes over. Gwendolyn Brooks tells us, "This is the urgency: Live! and have your blooming in the whirlwind." It's a nice thought to hang onto when you look around your home and see evidence of the whirlwind. At times like those, remember, too, the part about blooming.

Laundry

If you live with other people, develop a system for dealing with the laundry. Choose one day for laundry so that everyone knows just how long the clean clothes have to last. A large family might want two or three labeled laundry bins near the washer and dryer so that family members can deposit laundry by color or type of clothing. Those with clothing that needs ironing should do it themselves; this tends to encourage people to buy permanent press and other ironing-free items.

Tips

▶ A small hamper in each bedroom is a boon—unless the room's occupant discovers that the quickest way to "clean" the room is to throw everything in the hamper, whether it needs to be washed or not.

▶ A vertical washer-dryer combination will fit in most average closets, if you have trouble fitting a laundry space into your living area.

▶ Vacuum the dryer vent and the area around your dryer for greater energy efficiency and improved fire safety. Keep a wastebasket nearby for dryer lint; the trap needs to be emptied after each use.

▶ If you have a particularly heavily stained load of laundry, keep the lid up or halt the machine after it has filled and let the clothes soak in the soapy water—from five minutes to overnight.

▶ You and anyone whose laundry ends up in your washer need to always turn clothes right-side out (including, especially, socks) and empty all pockets before the item goes in a hamper.

▶ A swiveling rod that usually lies flat against the wall can be pulled out to hang items on as they come from the dryer.

Organizing Aids

▶ Fold-down ironing board

▶ Hampers

▶ Shelf for detergent, bleach, spot remover, softener, and coat hangers

▶ Stacking laundry bins

The "Home Office"

The business of daily life is a business: it generates paper, recordkeeping, and bookkeeping, sometimes in what seems like overflow amounts.

—C. L. KEYWORTH (1984)

"Home office" is in quotation marks here to distinguish it from a business that you operate from your home. For information about setting up that kind of office, see Chapter 7. However, every home today needs a spot dedicated to its business: the mail, bills, tax information, appliance warranties, school reports, medical information, insurance policies, personal information, magazine subscriptions, and much more.

At a minimum, you need a clear surface, a chair, and several paper trays. What is essential is to have a spot that is used solely for paperwork. If your space is really restricted, keep all paperwork organized in a large box that can be taken out from under the bed, for example, and worked on at the kitchen table, after which everything is returned to the box.

Some clever people have made efficient desk areas out of closets, installing shelving in the top half of the closet, one two-drawer file cabinet under a piece of wood mounted on stainless steel braces, a wall light, and a chair.

However you set it up, a place to take care of household business should include most of the following:

▶ Phone book, Rolodex file, address book, or computer address files

▶ Office staples: pens, marking pens, pencils, pencil sharpener, cellophane tape, stapler and staples and staple remover, paperclips, rubberbands, ruler, scissors, sticky-back notes, calculator, and letter opener

▶ Filing materials: folders and file holder

▶ Four labeled paper trays for sorting, for example, (1) bills, (2) letters, (3) urgent, and (4) everything else

▶ Mailing supplies: stationery, postcards, envelopes, postage stamps, postage scale, return address labels, and a selection of greeting cards

▶ Extras: telephone, dictionary, correction fluid, and computer and accessories

Tips

▶ If you're short on space, mount a telephone on the wall, or add a 50-foot cord to the nearest phone. The best solution is having cordless phones in the house and using a handset.

▶ To help set up a home filing system, sort your papers into piles and then put them into labeled file folders. Possible file headings include

  ● Banking and money

  ● Car

- Correspondence
- Credit cards
- Health
- House
- Insurance (car, home, medical, and umbrella)
- Medical records for each family member
- Records (passport, birth certificate, social security card)
- Subscriptions
- Taxes
- Travel
- Utilities
- Warranties and receipts

▶ Be stingy about keeping paper. There's no point in giving house room to something that can be entered on the computer (which you back up faithfully) or that can be found online when you want it or obtained from someone else.

▶ See Chapter 7 for more information on organizing an office.

Outdoors

To me the outdoors is what you must pass through in order to get from your apartment into a taxicab.

—FRAN LEBOWITZ (1978)

If you live in an apartment or condo, you get to skip this section and go organize something else.

Now that they're gone, it's safe to say that as much work as it is to maintain a yard, garage, decks, patios, or whatever constitutes your "outdoors," you reap incalculable joy, relaxation, and feelings of well-being in return.

Tips

▶ *Garage.* As always, you will zone the garage into areas, and like will go with like: car accessories, motor oil, antifreeze, refill fluids, jack, and other auto tools; hammers, screwdrivers, pliers, saws, power tools, nails and screws, maybe even a table saw, and all your other tools; lawnmower, grass seeder, garden tools, and soil amendments; bicycles, skateboards, basketballs, and toys; storage for such things as storm doors and windows; trash and recyclables. Too much for one garage? That's the problem with garages. Spend time studying your garage and noting solutions on a pad of paper. Here are some possibilities:

- Shelving and perhaps cabinetry are a must—how much and what kind will depend on your space and your needs. Label every storage unit by the kind of item that goes there so that everyone in the house knows where to find—and return—items.

- All gardening tools (rakes, hoes, and shovels as well as hand implements) can be kept in a rolling caddy so that you can have everything you need wherever you're working in the yard and so that, when you need every inch of space in the garage for a project you're working on, the caddy can be rolled outside for a few days.

- Be sure all lids on paint cans are airtight, and label each can with the date used, the rooms it was used for, where you bought it, and the precise number and paint color.

- Bikes can be hung on ceiling hooks when they are not in constant use. When they are in constant use, they will probably be everywhere. Ceiling hooks can also be used for keeping bungee cords, extension cords, and extra hoses together; to hang a kayak or canoe; or to get anything that isn't used regularly out of your way.

- Industrial-strength netting can be attached to garage walls and used to hold basketballs, baseball and football equipment, and other sports articles. It can also hold rags and car polish, holiday lights and decorations (if boxed carefully), and sturdy seasonal household items that you don't have room for in the house (for example, a turkey pan or your boxed collection of holiday cookie cutters).

- If it suits you, use color to delineate garage areas, either by painting the walls or by painting lines on the garage floor.

- Recycling has been adopted by many Americans, and some cities have their own bins for green refuse, household trash, and plastic or can recycling. If you are responsible for your own recycling, buy a set of matching bins and label them Newspapers, Magazines, Mail, Cans, Plastic, and Glass. If you go through a lot of cans, there are small can crushers.

● Cleaning the garage includes washing the garage windows; sweeping out the garage; spray cleaning trash cans and recycling bins inside and out and letting them dry outside with the lids off; sweeping, shoveling, or otherwise cleaning off the driveway; and removing oil stains from the garage floor. For the last, there are so many remedies online that you can choose whichever of them involves something that you have around the house (kitty litter, Coke, muriatic acid, Dawn dishsoap, Era liquid detergent, and dozens of other items are recommended).

> *Eating outdoors makes for good health and long life and good temper, everyone knows that.*
> —ELSIE DE WOLFE (1913)

▶ *Patios and decks.* Your choice of materials, paint or stain colors, outdoor furniture, grill, and accessories are relevant to organizing only insofar as you choose items that are difficult to ruin (sturdy, colorfast, and repairable) and easy to maintain. Be a good friend to yourself. While purchasing items that are pleasing to the eye, make sure that they won't be a burden to you in the future.

▶ *Yards.* How you feel about organizing Nature is up to you, but leaning toward the relaxed side seems a better choice, given the variables you have to deal with. Where you probably need a plan is in watering and feeding your flowers, trees, bushes, and grass. Somewhere on your list, you should mark the days when you tend to them. You may reach a point where it becomes automatic and you no longer need to remind yourself, but until then, keep it on your list to avoid losing the money and time represented by dead grass and shrubbery. It's also depressing.

The one yard-organizing element that is fun for the born organizer as well as being useful and functional is the marker that tells you what is planted there. The metal stakes and labels, with their indelible marking pen, are almost indestructible. If you have only three rosebushes, you probably don't need markers, but if you have a number of plants, they're a big help: (1) in the spring, you know what should be coming up there, (2) if it keels over, you can tell what the poor, burnt-up heap of leaves used to be, and (3) if you don't recognize the plant when it begins to leaf out, you can read the marker. The good organizer also has a computer list of everything ever planted, along with a description, growing instructions, the price paid, and where it was purchased. This doesn't need to be you, but it helps to see what works, what doesn't, and what you need to purchase to fill in bare spots.

If you use heavy-duty electrical extension cords for outdoor lighting or power tools, cover the ends, where the two cords meet, with specially made, inexpensive two-part housings that keep the connection watertight.

Sprucing up the yard includes mowing the grass and trimming the edges, sweeping or clearing walkways, trimming bushes and trees, cleaning doormats and replacing worn-out ones, perhaps pressure-washing the outside of the house as well as the decks and patios, weeding flower beds and adding fresh mulch, and turning the compost pile.

Organizing Aids

▶ Ceiling hooks

▶ Garden tool rolling cart

▶ Metal plant markers

▶ Netting

▶ Recycling bins

▶ Shelves

Organizing Your Family

Actually, organizing your family is a joke, right up there with herding cats. However, with some planning and a little psychology, the family can pull together to make the home more pleasant for everyone:

▶ Make it easy for family members to pick up, to put things back, to take responsibility, and to contribute to the common good. Nobody wants to be the family messer-upper, but people are often too busy or too thoughtless or too hurried to do the right thing. This chapter offers many ways to keep the house somewhat organized ("somewhat" is not a bad goal, given that real live people are involved), but, in general, make good use of labeled containers, labeled hooks, and labeled shelves so that it's obvious where things go. Keep jiffy cleaning materials near the places they are used. The person who has to hunt for a dustpan or a sponge or shower cleaner is simply not going to do the job.

▶ Get others to take ownership. If adults and children can help plan their areas of the house, choose their wall colors, tell you *their* way of keeping an area neat, contribute an organizing solution, or otherwise become invested in what's going on, they'll be more likely to consider the state of the home theirs instead of its belonging to whichever person in the family wears the "boss" hat. (Before giving children a range of choices, limit the choices to what is affordable and possible.)

Tips

▶ The most important organizing tool in a family home is a big wall calendar. Keep it in a central location, near a phone, and permanently attach a pencil or pen to it. On this calendar goes absolutely every appointment, outing, meeting, school or sports event, or activity that anyone in the family is participating in. (No work-related scheduling is included, unless it takes place during family hours or consists of someone traveling on business, which would also affect the family.) Without a big picture of the family and its activities as a whole, no one can accurately plan their own activities, decide who has which car when, know when to schedule a babysitter, or invite someone to dinner without—oops!—its turning out that everyone's busy but you. In a subtle way, too, it promotes family unity, cooperation, and compromise. Because it's neutral ("The calendar says . . ."), individuals are more likely to accept the idea that their activity has been superseded by someone else's.

> *What would happen to my illusion that I am a force for order in the home if I wasn't married to the only man north of the Tiber who is even untidier than I am?*
> —KATHARINE WHITEHORN
> (1976)

▶ When two or more people share a home, a chalkboard or dry-erase board for leaving reminders, questions, and information is indispensable. Put it next to the calendar. Children tend to accept chores more readily from a chalkboard than from the parent's own lips. If you don't like the looks of a chalkboard or you have insufficient wall space for one, mount a small one on the inside of a cupboard door or a larger one on the back of the kitchen door or the side of a refrigerator. If you have a broom closet or a separate pantry, the backs of those doors are also possibilities. Corkboard is useful, and it is flexible if you buy it in squares that can be arranged to fit the available space, but it means having paper, pencil, and stickpins handy.

▶ A family kitty can be both literal and metaphorical. In the literal sense, small amounts of money are left in a box for use by anyone in the household for emergencies. Suggest that everyone deposit their loose change in it. This practice allows you to discuss family cooperation in terms of everyone contributing to the family "kitty" (favors, chores, helping each other) so that instead of some people doing all the putting in and others doing all the taking out, there is a sharing of family responsibilities, each according to their means and abilities.

- A job jar sounds like a good idea, and for some people it is. If it works for you, this is how it works: anyone who lives there can jot a job on a slip of paper and put it into the jar. Slips are drawn on Saturday morning. Alternatively, one can draw a slip anytime during a calendar week. Some people use it only for their children, filling out the slips themselves with child-appropriate chores. The children draw one slip apiece and must do that job unless they can trade with a sibling.

> It is a mystery why adults expect perfection from children. Few grownups can get through a whole day without making a mistake.
> —MARCELENE COX (1943)

  If you use different paper colors for adults and children, everyone can participate. There is actually software for the family job jar, but it's likely that you can manage the old-fashioned way and save yourself $20.

- Try to mark off a homework area for children. Too often, homework is done in the child's bedroom, which works very well for some children, but not at all for others. Use the dining room or kitchen table, or set up a simple work space with a door on file cabinets, end tables, or bricks. Certain children feel less isolated when they are part of the family scene and are more likely to ask for assistance from parents and less likely to be watching television instead of taking care of their schoolwork. In addition to having a dedicated location for homework, try to have a regular time for doing it and a box of extra school supplies nearby (at least paper and pens and a dictionary).

- A house book is a handy reference. In a folder or three-ring notebook, place standard instructions for babysitters; information and phone numbers necessary in an emergency; phone numbers for relatives, neighbors, friends, the doctor, the veterinarian, the electrician, the plumber, and often-called local places of business; instructions for feeding pets; operating instructions for any temperamental appliance; and instructions for working the irrigation system or for watering the yard and houseplants. Keep the book in a central location, and take a few minutes at dinner one night to tell the family where it is and what it contains.

▶ Even small children (who love *real*, as opposed to make-believe, work) can help keep house. If you break chores down into small steps, many housekeeping tasks are teachable. Children can learn to set the table by matching items with a diagram of a place setting. They can make their own beds at a surprisingly young age (1) if you buy inexpensive bedspreads that are contoured to fit the bed or that have bold geometrics that give them something to align, and (2) if you never go in afterward and straighten up the bedspread. Set a timer for cleanup time and give each child a basket or bag or toy wagon to collect toys in. Other small, but important, chores for children are:

- They can set the breakfast table the night before.

- They can be given storage boxes and paint or markers, and allowed to label each box with the toys that belong in it.

- The night before, they can make part or all of the lunches for school or work.

- They can lay out their clothes for school the night before.

- They can carry their full hampers to the laundry once a week.

- As of first or second grade, most children can be taught to use a washing machine and learn a few simple rules (lights and darks) for washing their own clothes.

- They can sort laundry and deliver it to its owners.

- After school, they can make cold salads with simple ingredients for dinner side dishes; older children can prepare one meal a week, given some guidance.

- Raking leaves, shoveling snow, weeding, and watering the grass are all time-honored chores for young people.

- They can answer the phone correctly and take messages.

▶ Displaying inadequacy is an old trick: "But I don't know how to work the washing machine." "Who designed this coffeemaker? Nobody could figure it out." "But I'm just not good at dusting." This is a difficult argument to win because it's not that hard to look dumb. Which means that someone else has to do the job. If you find some of this going on around your house, cave in to whatever ignorance is expressed and ask the person to choose from among other chores of similar usefulness to the family.

▶ Keeping hydrated, especially in the summer, is a pastime with children. Figure out a way in which they can get water and other liquids by themselves—without, however, using every glass in the house. Sturdy aluminum glassware with each child's name stenciled on one glass will keep the glasses count down. Inexpensive large plastic beverage servers (under $20) can be set up in the morning and will probably need to be refilled only once.

▶ Keep a box or part of a drawer in the kitchen dedicated to often-used items like scissors, cellophane tape, marking pens, a stapler, a small screwdriver, and scratch paper. Otherwise, family members will be raiding your desk or toolbox for these items.

▶ A pet door is a timesaver if you have a dog like the great Outagain, who always wanted out again, but who, interestingly enough, always wanted in again quite as often.

▶ If some people's possessions get confused with other people's possessions, use a different color for each family member and either put a small dot of paint on the backside of an item or stitch an X in that color thread on an item of clothing. Color-coding sheets and towels for different bedrooms, bathrooms, and uses helps get the right items back to the right rooms.

▶ Depending on your feelings about it, a simple household rule that no food is allowed outside of the kitchen and perhaps the family room will take care of a lot of small detritus.

▶ A yard sale always seems like a good idea for defragmenting your home. If you're a social person and you'd enjoy chatting with people who stop by to look at your things, or if your children are excited about having one, go ahead. However, if you're looking to make a lot of money on stuff you don't need anyway, you'll probably be disappointed. If you're in a certain income tax bracket, you're better off donating everything and taking a tax credit for it. And it's easier and less time-consuming to do it that way. Everyone probably has to have at least one yard sale before they see that, no, this was not a good idea or, yes, this was great fun. If you do have one, make sure you schedule it on the preferred days in your area (Saturday is usually the most popular), advertise or post clear directions to your house, and do not overprice your items. People come to a sale looking for bargains. If they wanted to pay *that* much, they'd shop at a dollar store. To avoid marking every single item (especially if you have a great deal to sell), separate items into piles (on tables or on blankets) with signs like "Every item 25¢." Yes, some clever folks will try to say that they got their dollar item on the 25¢ table, but you should probably be able to deal with that.

▶ In general, use containers to group similar items. The silverware drawer should hold only silverware. The first-aid box, the office supplies shelf, the toy bins, and the photo albums should all contain what you would expect them to, and nothing else. If your household is fairly complex, and if you don't mind a little tackiness, invest in a label maker and label everything you can. Afterward, take your housemates on a tour to show them where everything goes.

▶ You can sometimes find family mailboxes at yard sales and spruce them up. But you might prefer to assemble ready-made cube boxes, which are much roomier, either to stand on the floor or to be wall-mounted (attached where there are wall studs), with one cube devoted to each family member for their mail, reminders, signed permission slips, books, notes, and misplaced personal items. If you have room, add an extra cube for each child's schoolwork and artwork, which will become voluminous by the end of the school year. At that time, go through the stack of papers with the child, weeding out the less significant pieces and boxing up the remainder with the year's date on it. Keep a pen and sticky-back notes nearby so that you can ask for the return of or add an explanation to an item. If your family doesn't usually have a cube's worth of mail, try a hanging vertical paper sorter. It mounts on the wall and takes up little space because the pockets are angled. Label each pocket with a family member's name. If you have other categories (take-out restaurant flyers, for example), you can snap on additional pockets.

► In *A Perfect Mess*, Eric Abrahamson and David H. Freedman write, "Mess in itself never seems to be a problem; it's the difference in how the two people view the state of order in their home that rankles." In achieving a somewhat organized home, compromises among the parties most concerned will be necessary (most people understand that children are anarchists and thus are less interested in being part of organizing anything that involves work). But Rita Mae Brown's advice is also realistic: "For you to be successful, sacrifices must be made. It's better that they are made by others but failing that, you'll have to make them yourself."

Organizing Aids

► Baskets

► Chalkboard or dry-erase board

► File folders

► Label printer

► Large calendar

► Marking pens

► Sticky-back notes

► Three-ring notebook

The House As a Whole

There is probably no thrill in life to compare with that of turning the key in one's first house or apartment.
—BELLE LIVINGSTONE (1959)

Some organizing strategies cut across rooms and areas. If you think of your house as a flowing, almost living organism, you can spot the places where things get jammed up.

Tips

► Set up an "outgoing" place near the door where you can put everything that will be leaving the house (books to go to the library, drycleaning to be dropped off, outgoing mail, checks to be deposited at the bank, a casserole dish to be returned to a neighbor, a birthday gift for a colleague). A large carryall is handy for collecting these items. Keep your briefcase here, too. If everything that's leaving the house is kept near the door, you're much less likely to forget any of it—and it won't be cluttering up the rest of the house.

> *Life is one long struggle to disinter oneself, to keep one's head above the accumulations, the ever-deepening layers of objects . . . which attempt to cover one over, steadily, almost irresistibly, like falling snow.*
> —ROSE MACAULAY (1936)

▶ Clean green and live green as much as you can. The health, environmental, and even financial benefits are many. Detergents, dishsoaps, multipurpose cleaners, and many other household items come in nontoxic, biodegradable, and environmentally friendly versions. Read labels carefully, however; some companies indulge in "greenwashing" (making false or misleading claims about the environmental virtues of a product or practice).

▶ Drawing up a household inventory is a nuisance, but if you start one early on, it's fairly simple to add items as you purchase them. Typically, you want to include the name of the item, a brief description, the date it was bought, the price paid, and any other information that would help to identify it or set it apart as unique. In addition to listing all your major possessions, videotape your home, identifying items with an oral commentary. The list plus the videotape will be invaluable to you if you should ever be faced with a catastrophe such as a theft, fire, or earthquake. It's also a good way to determine your homeowner's insurance needs.

▶ Rolling storage carts can be moved from room to room or from one part of a room to another and, for their size, hold quite a few items. They're particularly useful in the kitchen or office or anywhere you work on a hobby. When a cart outgrows its usefulness in one area, you'll probably find other good uses for that cart somewhere else.

▶ Whenever a room is painted, keep some of the paint in a clean jelly jar or other clear container and indicate the room it was used for. Keep these small jars of paint, along with some children's paint-brushes, in a cool, dry place. When you need to touch up a scratch or nail hole or other small paint defect, you'll be delighted not to have to dig out a big old gallon paint can, pry the lid off, and stir it for 10 minutes. And you're much more likely to touch up flaws if it's easy. In addition, keep your stir sticks—they'll have the color of the paint on them. On the clean end of the stick, mark the date and which room you used it for. You can take the stick with you when you're trying to match furnishings to the paint.

▶ Attractive straw baskets can keep small items from wandering. As people come in the door, a nearby basket can catch their car keys, which are then handy when they're ready to go out the door again. Baskets at the bottoms and tops of stairs can fill up with items going up or down. In living areas, baskets of current magazines look neat until it's time to carry the basket to the recycling bin and remove the oldest ones. A basket might be kept near the television with mending, repairs, knitting, or other minor, somewhat mindless, and not urgent tasks that can be done while chatting with someone or watching television or a movie. Be kind to yourself—when you put the broken piggy bank in there, add the proper glue and a rag so that you're all ready to go.

▶ Always add needed supplies to the shopping list *before* you are down to the last one or two. This means that you won't have to make emergency runs or feel pressured about getting to the store. Some homes never run out of anything. It's apparently possible.

▶ Replace the batteries in your smoke detectors every year (but also check the batteries in your hardwired, battery backup detectors once a month). Most people are unaware that the U.S. Fire Administration recommends that the entire smoke detector (both battery-operated and hardwired types) should be replaced every eight to ten years. Check the label on the back for the manufacturing date and then write the replacement date with a marker so that when you change the batteries each year, you'll be reminded. Tie your yearly battery-changing date to some significant date so that it's easier to remember—Valentine's Day because you love your family; Halloween because it's scary to think of a fire in your home; July 4 because of "fire" works. For good information on smoke detectors, see the U.S. Fire Administration Web site (www.usfa.dhs.gov).

▶ Erma Bombeck once asked, "If the nest is truly empty, who owns all this junk?" Most organizers will suggest not keeping items for young adult children who are living away from home. For most people, that's easier said than done. The best compromise is to tell your adult children that you'll keep their favorite things until they get their first home with extra space *if* they will pull them all together and box them up with their name on it. You'll then have to bite the bullet and store their boxes under a bed, in the attic or basement, or in the closet of their old room—now your guest room. You're still giving their stuff house room, but it's out of your way and ready for transport when the day arrives.

▶ Choose an overcast day for washing windows, as bright sunlight will dry the glass cleaner too quickly, leaving streaks. First soak paint drips, gluey labels, and those mysterious spots that no one can account for with a mixture of shampoo and warm water, and then scrape them with a putty knife, being careful not to scratch the glass. Using a commercial window-washing solution or your own (1 gallon water + 1 teaspoon baby shampoo or 1 gallon water + 1 1/2 cups of vinegar or 1 gallon warm water + a few drops of dishwashing liquid), wash the windows with a microfiber cloth (you can get a pack of 20 for less than $10 at Costco in the auto section) and dry them immediately with a soft cloth. You can also use a squeegee with a good rubber edge. Work vertically on one side of the windows (inside or outside) and horizontally on the other, so that you can tell which side has a streak.

▶ Even if you don't have cats or dogs, a lint brush (some work markedly better than others) is a handy item to have for spot-cleaning furniture and for picking up those minute clinging bits on rugs that even the best vacuum can't seem to handle.

▶ Attaching casters to some pieces of furniture allows you to rearrange a room in seconds to accommodate visitors or special activities. Furniture leg pads that allow you to move even the heaviest furniture on wood floors (one type of pad) or carpeting (a smooth pad) if you need to adapt furniture for different room uses are also available.

▶ When space is at a premium, consider pocket doors that take up no floor or room space but slide into walls. Also, sometimes rehanging a door in the opposite direction opens up the space that was needed to open the door; a door opening into a hallway takes less needed space than one that opens into a bedroom, for example.

▶ If you often have overnight guests, be prepared with an attractive basket containing an extra house key; sample-size soaps, shampoos, and other notions; maps and brochures from your area; a "Do Not Disturb" sign; a night-light; and perhaps a flashlight. Their room should have empty hangers, a set of towels, a decent reading lamp, and a luggage rack or a chair that can serve as one.

▶ "Spring cleaning" can be done anytime. Start by walking around the house with a notepad and pen. In each room, (1) make a pile of everything that belongs in another room in the house, (2) make a pile of everything that is not being used and doesn't appear likely ever to be used, and (3) jot down what the room needs in the way of cleaning (wash and iron curtains, wash windows, touch up paint, organize closet, dryclean bedspread, and so on). Distribute the misplaced items, put the Give-Away items in a box or bag by the front door to be taken to a donation center, and type up your complete list. Make secondary lists of all like items; for example, everything that needs to be drycleaned should go in one list so that you don't forget any items when you're collecting for the drycleaners. All the rooms that need their windows washed go on another short list so that once you have your window-washing equipment out, you won't forget a room. First do items that involve other people or machines (drop off the drycleaning; start a load of laundry; drop off an appliance at the repair shop; call for the Salvation Army to pick up the old bunk beds) so that these jobs can be getting done while you're working. Then focus on one room at a time, leaving yourself space for a little R&R so that you don't get overwhelmed and decide that next year will do as well. In your big cleaning, don't forget to replace the air filters in furnaces and air conditioners, to check your chimney, and to clean out rain gutters.

▶ If you keep your sewing machine threaded with clear nylon thread, you can repair most of the things in your mending pile without having to change thread colors.

▶ At some point, you may be faced with having more items than your home can conveniently handle, and your thoughts naturally turn to . . . self-storage. Apparently one in ten U.S. families rents self-storage space, amounting to 2.2 billion square feet nationwide. (Of the 58,000 storage facilities around the world, 52,000 are in the United States.) Unmaintained storage units have given rise to storage auctions. How important could these items have been if people are able to abandon them? Don Aslett, who possibly introduced the word *clutter* to popular culture in 1984, calls storage units "the ghost towns of clutter." Unless you are renting very short-term (you're moving or you have excess inventory), avoid this route if you can. It is a slippery slope, leading to more storage units. It is expensive. And it may be unnecessary.

▶ To keep items out of sight in the living room or in a bedroom or study, a small round table with a floor-length cloth will serve as an end table or lamp table while hiding under its skirts boxes of craft materials, stacks of books, or other items that are not used daily.

▶ If areas of the house feel small to you, consider self-adhesive mirror tiles. They take up virtually no space and expand the visual sense of a room.

▶ Drawer dividers and compartmented desk trays—plastic, wood, or rubber—have multiple uses in keeping the contents of drawers where they belong.

▶ If your apartment or home still has old-fashioned radiators, you can use the dead space above them for narrow wall-mounted shelves, or even fit a cover on top of the radiator to use as a shelf. (The latter is iffy; make sure that you're not impeding heat flow and that the cover doesn't become too hot.)

▶ Use the tops of tall furniture (china cabinet, bookshelves, kitchen cabinets, display cabinets, and desk hutches) for either art objects or attractive boxes of items that are not used often.

▶ If you've read this book this far, you know what's involved in dealing with attics and basements: zoning, sorting like with like, and labeling airtight boxes and bins. If you keep luggage in the attic, place the smallest piece inside the next smallest piece, and so on, until you have placed as much luggage as possible inside other pieces. Heavy-duty garbage bags can then protect the largest pieces from dust and that special look that luggage gets when it's been in an attic for a long time.

▶ You can use narrow rolling shelves, like the one suggested for use in the kitchen, in the laundry between washer and dryer, in the study between desk and file cabinet, or in bedroom closets. Several kinds and sizes are available. If you only have a few inches to spare, this might be your solution.

▶ If you haven't got a linen closet, keep sheets (fold them inside one of their matching pillowcases) and blankets on the closet shelf of the bedroom in which they're used; keep towels in a wall cabinet or on shelves in the bathroom. Tablecloths, placemats, and napkins can be hung in a closet over padded hangers or from clip-type hangers.

▶ If you're cramped for space, take a walk around with a creative eye. In some homes, you might find an interior hollow space under or next to a staircase that could be turned into a closet. Look for unusual places to hang shelving (high up under the ceiling, for example). If two children share a room, a bookcase room divider won't take much space from either half, but will give the feeling of private rooms while providing shelf storage.

▶ A house will appear more organized if you keep the surfaces cleared off, choose organizing elements (bookshelves, baskets, and boxes) in the same background color, and restrict projects or messes to one area of a room. A group of the same kind of labeled stacking drawers, rather than a chest here, a bin there, and a straw basket somewhere else, will give a room a streamlined look.

▶ Somewhere in the house—the attic, the linen closet, the front hall closet, your bedroom closet—stash a box with gift-wrapping paper, ribbons, scissors, tape, gift cards, and any gifts you manage to squirrel away. You'll love yourself for keeping it all in one place when you have to prepare a gift.

Organizing Aids

► Baskets

► Carryall

► Casters

► Drawer dividers

► Green cleaning products

► Microfiber auto cloths (excellent for all kinds of cleaning, including computer monitors; do not wash them, however, with powdered detergent, which may remain and then scratch surfaces, or with softening agents, which may cut their effectiveness)

► Pocket doors

► Rolling storage carts

► Shelving

► Stanton carts (www.homedecorators.com) are nice-looking wheeled chests that come in many heights, several widths, varying numbers of drawers, and your choice of finish; they'll hold scrapbooking and craft materials, jewelry, maps, papers, or anything else that you want to keep organized and out of sight

Moving

With any luck, you do not move that often. Once is actually quite enough. The only thing that gets anyone through a move is looking forward to the new, and presumably better, situation.

He moves a great deal. So often . . . that every time he comes out into his backyard the chickens lie down and cross their legs, ready to be tied up again.
—ZORA NEALE HURSTON (1979)

Tips

► As soon as you think you're moving, go through the house and start stripping it of absolutely everything that does not have a place in your new home.

- Some things will be junk—it's hard to admit, but there you are. Some people have so much after years of living in a home that they rent a dumpster for all the rusty hamster cages, pieces of brick, replaced screens, broken aquariums, bits of lumber, and other detritus that they have somehow overlooked for years.

- Other things must be returned to their owners, like it or not. Your now-balding brother who left a box of college books with you many years ago must take responsibility. Your young adult children may try changing their addresses, but if you are clever, you will be able to send them their boxed possessions that you've been keeping. The friend who asked you to store her baby crib—out of fear of attracting a baby to it—is now well past her childbearing years and must come take it back.

- You can, of course, have a yard sale, but only if you love doing this and you have a great many things to get rid of. Otherwise, it's less time-consuming to call Goodwill or the Salvation Army to pick up any decent pieces of furniture and for you to take the smaller items to a donation center. With any luck, a nearby nonprofit group will be trying to raise money and will come collect vans full of your unwanted items for its sale. A tax donation slip will probably net you more real money than a yard sale.

► Almost as soon as you start stripping, take every possible measurement of your new living quarters and make a list of the items that will remain for your use (blinds, light fixtures, built-in kitchen desk). Over and over, you will need to know if this table fits where you want it to, if that desk can be gotten through a door, if the bookshelves are too tall for the new house, or if the ceiling light is needed. These measurements and this list will be a great help in stripping your present house, as you will be able to see what will not fit and what you need to keep. By the time you've gotten rid of everything that you won't need at the new home, you're ready to start packing.

▶ Make two lists: everything that needs to be done to move you out of your present home and everything that needs to be done to move you into your new home. Your lists will be unique to you and much longer than these, but here are some items to get you started:

- Present house: cancel phone and Internet service, electrical service, gas or propane service, and newspaper (or change address, if local); sign up for mail-forwarding service with the U.S. Postal Service; send new-address notices to friends, relatives, colleagues, and magazines that you subscribe to; cancel or transfer your cable or satellite television service; do all the repairs mandated by your real estate contract; keep track of the various inspections needed to ensure the sale of the house; make sure that you have the necessary funds available for the closing; start collecting sturdy moving boxes or buy them (if you aren't having professional movers); pack everything up (you or movers); and give the house a final cleaning after your things are out.

- New house: set up phone, electrical, gas, Internet, newspaper, and other services; if possible, do all cleaning and painting and major repairs before your furniture arrives; unpack (may take months); enjoy.

▶ The U.S. Postal Service's online site allows you to have your mail forwarded to your new address. To do this, you'll need a valid e-mail address and a valid credit card whose billing address matches either the address you're moving from or the address you're moving to.

Organizing Aids

▶ Change-of-address cards
▶ Sturdy boxes

CHAPTER 10

How to Organize Your Papers

*Tidied all my papers. Tore up and
ruthlessly destroyed much. This is always
a great satisfaction.*

—KATHERINE MANSFIELD (1922)

Every office needs some dedicated space or containers for papers. We
tend to think immediately of file cabinets, and they are certainly the
standard solution for safeguarding our papers. Today, however,
because of computers, we are generating less paper than we did several
decades ago.

Options for paper organizing range from the lowly accordion file to the
upright four-drawer file cabinet, through lateral and open-shelf files,
rolling file racks, vertical file pockets, and wall storage units. Your filing
accommodations may have come with your office, or you may be restricted
by the amount of space you have, so you may not have much choice. If you
do, however, assess your paper needs before investing in filing solutions—
you may need smaller accommodations than you think.

Principles

▶ Keep all papers in the same area of your office or in the same room in
your house. This is essential. Always do your paper handling in the
same place.

- Papers come in two basic kinds:

  - *Active.* These are also called working papers, pending papers, in-progress papers, current papers, or dynamic papers; they are papers that you are working with, about to work with, or waiting for something to happen with—in other words, papers that need a response from you. They include bills and letters as well as all business-related items.

  - *Passive.* You can't throw these away because you need to keep a record or because you may need to refer to them again, but they aren't going anywhere. These are also called reference files, archive files, inactive files, history files, permanent files, or storage files. In fact, you could divide them into files that you keep in your office because you may need to refer to them again and files that you have boxed up and put in storage. (Be cautious about storing anything but papers with tax, financial, or legal implications; you may not truly need them.)

- Papers need somewhere to land when they hit your desk. Choose a system that is convenient for you so that you'll use it. For example, you could have a set of four stacked paper trays labeled with your four main paper destinations:

  - To Be Filed
  - Outgoing
  - To Do
  - Urgent

And never forget that most important fifth paper "file": the wastebasket.

Because you have your own way of doing things, you might want, for example, a paper tray labeled Correspondence or, if this is one of your responsibilities, Bills. You

> *The real cause of a paperwork crisis is a problem with decision making; picking up the same piece of paper five times and putting it down again because you can't decide what to do with it.*
> —STEPHANIE WINSTON (1983)

don't want too many trays on your desk. Outgoing and To Be Filed seem fairly basic. Other than that, it's up to you to know which labels will push which of your buttons the right way.

▶ Every piece of paper needs a response. Of course, the response is often to toss it away. But that's actually one of the most important responses you can make. Not throwing something away means that it's going to sit with important papers and make for clutter and confusion. Here are your responses:

- Toss it away (or recycle it).

- Pass it on if it properly belongs to someone else or if you are going to delegate the responsibility for it (attach a sticky-back note with the name of the person it's going to and put it in your outbox).

- Act on it immediately (jot an answer right on the letter, put it in an envelope, address it, and put it in your outbox; send a brief, immediate e-mail response; leave a telephone message giving your response).

- File it in one of the paper trays on your desk, if you need to work on it further, or in your passive files, if it's simply FYI or a confirmation or something that needs no response.

▶ Unless you have a reason not to, check to see that all papers and notes are dated. In the case of incoming papers or letters that are dated when they were originated, note when you received them. Even if you write yourself a note, add the date—you might need to know that.

▶ Make room in your office for articles, newspapers, journals, magazines, books, and any other reading material needed for your work. You can use a

Where's my tax form? Where's the file that's supposed to hold my W-2 form and interest statement? Where's the mileage log I specifically asked be kept last year?? Where's the monthly check summary? And who's been stuffing Visa receipts in the aluminum foil drawer??!! How embarrassing. I'm surrounded by idiots and I'm the only one in the office.
—CATHY GUISEWITE (1987)

wooden paper tray, a magazine rack, vertical files, a shelf, or a straw basket. But keep these things off your desk (unless, of course, one of them is something that you need to be dealing with right now) so that they don't overwhelm you. If it helps, nobody today keeps up with what they "ought" to keep up with. You deal with your reading in 5-minute, 10-minute, or 30-minute increments when you're waiting, need to switch your brain off for a few minutes, or find yourself with an unexpected break. Keep the reading by the door so that on your way out, you can pick up an article or two to read while you're at the dentist, waiting for a meeting, or arriving early for an appointment.

Mail

▶ Always open mail next to a wastebasket and a recycling bin, and perhaps a shredder. You should be able to dispose of a good percentage of it seconds after it arrives in your office.

▶ Jot a keyword or two on a sticky-back note so that you won't have to reread a letter to know what to do with it. Avoid putting sticky-back notes on papers that are to be filed, however; they too often come off and are found nowhere near anything relevant. Pencil a note on the paper instead.

▶ Take immediate action on as much of the incoming mail as you can. Your guideline should be that if you can respond to a letter in less than five minutes, you'll save twice that by doing it now because you won't have to reread the letter and recall your reaction to it. It also hasn't been occupying a small part of your brain as something that needs to be taken care of.

▶ See Chapter 5 for more tips on dealing with mail.

Filing

The entire point of filing anything is to be able to find it again. Sometimes we think of filing as keeping things safe, or organized, or out of the way. In fact, we care about only one thing: how will we find this again if we need it?

Disorganized files have one (or more) of three basic problems:

- You haven't kept up with the filing, so your "files" consist of neat file drawers on top of which stacks of unfiled papers totter and sway.
- Unable to discard any paper, you have filed absolutely everything until your files are bulging with material you'll never touch again.
- Indecisive, you have worried over where to put this paper or that paper until finally you have put it any old where just to be done with it. You may never find these papers again.

> *One person's mess is merely another person's filing system.*
> —Margo Kaufman (1992)

Whether you are starting from scratch to organize your filing system or trying to make sense of old files, you need an overall plan. Before you start looking at files and get bogged down in what may be yesterday's miscalculations, consider your work or your life.

Break down your needs and interests into categories. Outline your headings on paper or on a computer before you actually create the files. What kinds of papers will you be dealing with? If it's a home office, you might consider broad categories like:

- Banking
- Car (maintenance, warranties, and so on)
- Credit cards
- Health, Brian
- Health, Chrissy
- Health, Jan
- Insurance, auto
- Insurance, homeowner's
- Insurance, life
- Insurance, medical
- Insurance, umbrella

- Manuals (camera, vacuum, and so on)
- Records (social security cards, birth certificates)
- Taxes
- Tuition
- Utilities—warranties and receipts

Or, you can put all the insurance information in one folder, put all the health records in another folder, and create other categories that your family uses.

Two caveats. (1) Most data (for example, bank account numbers, health histories, insurance ID numbers, and listings of tax deductions) should be input into your computer, where they are readily accessible, and backed up regularly. Files should be reserved for those papers for which you need a hard copy, such as credit card bills and tuition receipts. (2) Your hard (noncomputer) files need to be cleaned out once a year. At that time, you bundle up the credit card receipts, put a rubber band around them, print the year in bright red, and store them with the previous years' receipts. Ditto for the year's medical insurance records, the year's utility bills, and the year's bank account statements. Storing can be as simple as a brown paper bag in the attic or as fancy as colorful bins in a dry place in the garage.

For work files, break down your major headings by clients (Jacobs, Moorhen, Price), by years (2008, 2009), by projects (Cerium, Plutonium, Hydrogen), by functions (billing, accounting, reports, correspondence), by job responsibilities (menus, catering, linens), by geography (Wisconsin, Florida), or by other specific-to-you categories or combinations of several categories.

Which Papers Can Be Tossed?

The ability to achieve goals is directly related to a willingness to use the wastebasket.

—BARBARA HEMPHILL (1992)

Barbara Hemphill, CEO of the Hemphill Institute, an organizational consulting company with nationwide consultants, is also widely known for cautioning us that "Eighty percent of what we save, we never use."

The difference between papers that we absolutely must keep or we risk serving time for income tax irregularities and the papers that are clogging our filing arteries is a blurry distinction for most of us. "Better safe than sorry," we've been taught.

Some types of papers that can be discarded are:

▶ Duplicate material (why do we always make more copies than we need?)

▶ Outdated information and expired warranties

▶ Early versions of a finished project that no longer serve any purpose

▶ Information that you know you can find online

▶ Company reports that can be obtained from another department if necessary

▶ Pages and pages that you're saving because there's an address you might want—input the address into your computer and toss the papers

▶ Information that you found online and printed out; toss it—you can always find it online again

▶ Material that you know you have on your hard drive (which is also backed up)

▶ Articles about something that once interested you, but that you're unlikely to pursue any time soon; in any case, it will be old by then

▶ Letters that say nothing but "thanks for your letter" or something equally unimportant

Some types of papers that should be kept are:

▶ Records (birth, adoption, military service, marriage, divorce, citizenship, death)

▶ Things that are irreplaceable or would be time-consuming to replace (social security card, newspaper clipping of your parents' wedding)

▶ Evidence of ownership (car title, house deed, patents, copyrights)

- ▶ Tax returns and supporting documents
- ▶ Receipts for major purchases
- ▶ Things that are needed for redemption (insurance, retirement, pensions, investments, stocks, bonds)
- ▶ Original copies of wills, living wills, powers of attorney, and contracts

The documents that are important enough to keep are important enough to keep very securely. Traditional options are a safe-deposit box or a fireproof home safe. A clever newcomer is the PortaVault (www.securitaonline.com), a heavy-duty, water-resistant canvas bag that can store 100 vital records in plastic sleeves so that in case of emergency, you can grab the bag and have access to all important records.

Kimberley Lankford, of *Kiplinger*, says that you'll want to keep tax returns forever. And you should keep supporting material for your tax returns for at least six years—after which the IRS can no longer knock on your door to complain that you've underpaid by at least 25 percent. On the other hand, there is no limit at all on fraud, so if you've been playing games, you'll have to keep all your tax material forever. There is good online information on keeping records (payments to retirement funds, investments, and so on). Check there for an idea of how long to save which papers, and then run the answer by the IRS or an accountant.

Tips

- ▶ When you are filing, open up all folded papers, brochures, and letters; staple loose sheets that belong together; and always put the new item *either* in the front of the file facing forward *or* in the back of the file facing backward (but be consistent), so that when you open a file, the contents are in rough chronological order.
- ▶ A tickler file is a way of keeping track of items with deadlines or dates attached. You can have a linear computer file (see Chapter 3), or you can have a physical file. Use an accordion file with 12 pockets (print the months of the year on the tabs) or 31 pockets (number from 1 to 31 for the days of the month). In the first case, you slip into the January pocket bills to be paid that month, your estimated tax

forms, birthday cards or RSVPs to be sent, and anything else that you need to take care of in January. In the second case, into the 1 pocket goes a card that must be mailed on that date to reach a colleague on the third of the month, a note to call someone on that day, or anything else that you might need to take care of. It seems more efficient—less paper is needed and less space is taken up—to keep all dated items in a list on your computer. Then, instead of rummaging around in the "January" pocket to see what needs to be taken care of first, you can go down the list and see what's coming up. It is, of course, a personal choice, but you definitely need a system for keeping track of what is coming due when.

▶ Sometimes creating a new file is just enough trouble that we drop papers into a file that's "near enough" in subject matter. You're probably going to have trouble finding those particular papers. Instead, keep a handful of folders, labels, tabs, and marking pens— whatever you use—right in the back of your top file drawer so that you are never more than seconds away from making a file that *will* be easy to find.

▶ A desk with built-in file drawers (usually one deep file drawer on each side of the desk with standard desk drawers on top of them) or a door-sized piece of wood atop two double-drawer file cabinets (the longtime favorite of home offices and college students) is handier than you might think. Even if you have extensive files, keeping the folders you use most often in those desk drawers means that it takes you only seconds to drop a paper into a file folder without even leaving your chair.

▶ If coworkers or family members use your files, explain and demonstrate your system to them. You might also keep a typed index in the front of each file drawer listing the files to be found there (and, when necessary, some of the key items in each file). If others are notoriously poor at returning papers to the proper file, leave a paper tray on or near the file cabinet so that you can refile them yourself. It's extra work, yes, but at least you'll be able to find things again. (If you have more files than the average bear, you might need file indexing software instead of a manual index.)

- Many organizing experts recommend handling each piece of paper only once. Because this isn't always possible in the real world, focus instead on never putting a paper back where you picked it up from if you can get it to its proper home in less than a couple of minutes.

- Always shred discarded papers containing your social security, credit card, or other important numbers that can be used by identity thieves. If you don't have room for a shredder or don't have many papers to shred, at least buy a shredding scissors.

- Staple papers together when you're filing. Paper clips get jammed or pulled off.

- When a trip or report or project is completed, gather together all the materials pertaining to it. After returning books or other materials to their owners, see what data you can save on the computer, allowing you, for example, to toss all the correspondence from the travel bureau except for its name and address and receipts for tax purposes. Sometimes there's just one bit of information on two or three sheets of paper; transfer the important datum to your computer, and discard the papers. When you've whittled down the material to just those items that need to be preserved for financial, legal, or personal reasons, you're ready to put that file in storage. (Remember to clean your computer files for this project at the same time because you can eliminate duplicate material that appears both in hard copy and on your computer.)

- If you need to "file" items that don't fit into file folders, you were born in the right century. Organizing accessories will keep tidy such disparate items as catalogs, journals, photos, maps, product samples, posters, brochures, bumper stickers, and cat toys. And then there are binders in which you can store odd-sized items like clippings.

- Colored plastic envelopes for $8^1/_2 \times 11''$ papers help you spot filed materials that you refer to most often.

- When you're filing a paper, notice whether it's something you can discard after a certain time (for example, a warranty that expires in a year). With a heavy black marker, indicate in the upper right-hand corner the date on which you can toss it. As you go about your regular filing, you can riffle through a file to see if any black dates catch your eye.

► Barbara Hemphill once said, "There are basically two kinds of tax-payers—those who feel comfortable only if they record deductions as they occur during the year and those who prefer to ignore the entire issue until the fear of the penalty for late payment is greater than their willingness to procrastinate." If you can afford it, and sometimes even if you think you can't afford it, paying a reputable professional to do your taxes is a "best buy." In that case, the most important thing you can do is keep all tax-related papers in the same place. It's nice if you can organize them in categories, but just having them all in a box, in whatever fashion, will make you happy at least once a year. Filing tax returns is the subject of many good books; if you take care of your own taxes, you'll need to read them and keep up to date on the changes every year. A combination of running paper and computer files should be kept. Keep a large manila envelope or file folder boldly labeled "Taxes" in a convenient drawer, and keep all receipts and tax information there. At the same time, keep a running log in a computer file of everything you keep track of: income, property taxes, sales tax, deductible items, charitable donations, utility bills, and homeowner's insurance (if you deduct for a home office, for example). When it is time to calculate your taxes, between the large envelope, your computer file, some tax software, and a good tax reference book, you'll be set

► If you don't have many files, consider stacking file drawers or file boxes or accordion files that sit on a shelf. Especially for current work, it's handy to be able to just drop a paper into a file in an open box (put the lid on it when you're ready to store it).

► Getting down and dirty: if you have piles of papers to sort, there's really only one good place to do it: the floor. Start making piles of like items, labeling each pile with a sticky-back note (for example, "Rheinmann case"). At first, sort very narrowly. Later you can collapse several piles under one umbrella topic (if they seem to go together). Your one thought, your one question is, under what word would I look to find this? *Rheinmann* is easy. Some others will be more complicated. Maybe there are only five sheets of paper destined for one file. Normally, such a thin file might not be worth its keep.

But if you know that the only way you're going to find those five pages again is by looking under that word, then they need their own file. Always work with a keyword that brings to mind a particular document. Conversely, when you look at that document, what keyword comes to mind?

► If filing is your pet peeve, you might like to join (for free) the popular I Hate Filing Club (www.pendaflex.com), established in 1986. If you forget the URL, don't worry, just Google "I Hate Filing Club." The site offers a community of like-minded people (100,000 of them), helpful suggestions, and even coupons for Pendaflex file folders.

Organizing Aids

► *Folders.* Most people prefer hanging file folders because they don't go limp and sink into crevices in the file drawer. They come with plastic tabs into which you can slip a label. It's easier to read through the clear tabs, but they come in colors if you want to color-code your files. Experiment for yourself, but if you can print the file titles neatly with a heavy black felt-tip pen, you'll be able to read the labels more easily than if you type them. Most people automatically put the tab at the back of the file, as you find them on simple file folders, but you can insert the file with the label to the front. That way, when you pull the label toward you, the file opens up to allow you to get what you need, usually without your having to remove the folder.

► *Highlighters.* Some individuals don't like writing on original documents, but if they are for your own use, you'll find it extremely helpful to yourself to highlight a few keywords when you are familiar with the document. Otherwise, months later, you would have to read the entire thing to extract the important parts.

CHAPTER 11

How to Organize Your Computer

I don't have a computer. I'm going to wait until
that whole fad is over. I was suckered in on the
Pet Rock. Not twice, people.

—KATHLEEN MADIGAN (2004)

Computers have overturned our ideas about time and effectiveness. They allow us to work at speeds and with an efficiency unimagined only decades ago.

Contemporary humans are exposed to more facts in a single day than medieval people faced in a lifetime. Although we've yet to realize the full implications of our accelerated culture, one thing is certain: "As the clock once revolutionized work and society, the computer is reconstructing how we work and live with time" (Diana Hunt and Pam Hait, 1990). But computers are like Henry Wadsworth Longfellow's little girl:

There was a little girl,

Who had a little curl,

Right in the middle of her forehead.

When she was good,

She was very good indeed,

But when she was bad she was horrid.

When a computer goes bad, "horrid" is an egregious understatement.

Protecting Your Data

Even more important than organizing your computer files is keeping them safe. Messy files you can work with. Disappeared files? Not so easily.

In addition to technical problems, which can be taken care of by online or technical support, two things can "go bad" with a computer. A virus can infect it, destroying, corrupting, and otherwise making nonsense of your data; or it can crash. "Crash" covers a variety of happenings, but they all come down to the same thing: you've lost everything you had on your computer.

> *The world is divided into two groups of people: those who have lost data, and those who are about to.*
> —STEPHANIE WINSTON (1994)

You may sometimes be able to recover data with the help of experts, but it's going to take time and it's going to cost money. In the meantime, you don't have access to, basically, your life.

You protect the data on your computer in two ways:

► You invest in a reliable backup system and, if it's not automatic, you back up your computer at least once a day. Look into the options available to you (external or internal drive, writable CD or DVD, flash drive, tape, and online offsite backup service) and find the one that you will use. No matter how good a backup system appears to be, if you don't use it, it's worthless. Make a second copy of backed-up but irreplaceable files on CDs or DVDs and store them away from the office (even if you use an offsite service, it's good to have a second set of critical files in a secure place). Label the CDs with title and date.

> *I've gotten much better at the computer: When it goes bonkers, I regain consciousness much faster than before.*
> —MARIE SHEAR (2001)

► You invest in reliable antivirus and antispyware software. Never let it expire. Either sign up for automatic renewal via credit card or note in your tickler file when it's time to renew. Every six months or so, do a little research online to make sure that what you have is still top-of-the-line. In the meantime, set your antivirus and antispyware protection to update at least once a day and run a full-system scan at least once a week. Don't wait for a disaster to make you a believer.

Passwords

You can "lose" data a third way, but you don't know it for a while. Your computer appears to be in good order, but someone has managed to get past your passwords and has stolen personal, defining information about you—information that is used by identity thieves.

> *His personal opinion was that if you wanted sensitive information to get out, you put it in a computer.*
> —LINDA HOWARD (1998)

Your credit cards are susceptible, whether or not you use them for online purchases. In fact, any of your online financial information—bank accounts, credit card statements, online billing services—is vulnerable. Hackers have demonstrated in the past that they can get into some otherwise very secure institutions.

You have two choices: live in fear and trepidation, or take some precautions while also keeping a close eye on your credit rating, credit cards, and bank accounts.

> *You can steal a lot more with a computer than with a gun.*
> —GINA SMITH (1997)

- ▶ Deal only with reputable online sites.
- ▶ Use a separate e-mail address for purchases.
- ▶ Notify the three main credit bureaus that they are to contact you any time an attempt is made to open a new account in your name.

Select strong but flexible passwords. Geek Squad agent Derek Meister suggests combining letters and numbers to create a base password, to which you can add a suffix for each site you use. Do not use your birth date, your social security number, or your address for the base password, but if you have a poor memory, use something that you can remember. Perhaps you had a memorable trip to Morocco in 2007. Your base password would be MOR2007. Your eBay password is then MOR2007eb, and your Amazon password is MOR2007am.

Organizing Computer Files

Despite differences between and among PCs and Macs, a few organizing guidelines—together with a good reading of your hardware and software manuals—will help you keep your computer files tidy and efficient.

▶ Partition your hard drive or, if that's not possible or desirable for you, at least think of and work with your computer as consisting of three distinct types of files:

- All your software program files, from utilities to word processing and spreadsheets to graphics, games, and music

- Your active (or current) files

- Your stored (or reference) files

If you actually partition your drive, you then need to back up only your active files (unless you add programs to the first group or files to the third group), which will, over the long run, save you a lot of time. In addition, when you keep working files and program files separate, you're not likely to inadvertently lose active files when you install or upgrade programs.

▶ *Storage files.* Keeping completed work out of your way in storage files facilitates your work with active files. As soon as you finish a project or a series of files, check for duplicate and unnecessary material and then transfer the remaining files to storage. If you haven't partitioned your drive, give all storage files names beginning with Z so that they fall together.

▶ *Active files.* For active files, (1) choose a broad subject or category heading for each main folder; (2) identify subcategories for the files in each folder; (3) always group like with like because a folder contains, by definition, files and possibly other folders (which then contain files); and (4) organize folders and files in the old outline format. For example:

I. Leatheringham Co.
    A. Legal
        1. Contracts
        2. Mediation
        3. Correspondence
    B. Construction
        1. Architect
        2. Contractor
        3. Advertising
        4. Correspondence
           a. Aventon
           b. Marshall
              i. Marsh2007
              ii. Marsh2008

II. Travel
    A. London
        1. 030808
        2. 032108
        3. 042908
    B. Edinburgh
        1. 070108
        2. 081008

III. Continuing Ed
    A. Accounting 201
        1. Midterm
        2. Final
    B. Accounting 301
        1. Midterm
        2. Final
    C. Records

You don't, of course, use the numerals and letters, but think in those terms: what subjects belong under which other subjects? Although you can do it, some experts recommend not going more than three subfolders deep because you may have trouble recalling where a sub-sub-sub-subfolder is. However, if your plan is logical (to you), you'll probably be able to find it.

> *There's a proverb which says "To err is human" but a human error is nothing to what a computer can do if it tries.*
> —AGATHA CHRISTIE (1969)

- ▶ *Naming files.* If you Google "naming files," you'll find pages and pages of discussions, suggestions, and naming systems that work for their users. What's important is to find your own system—it must be based on the kind of work you do and, most important, on how you are going to locate folders and files later on. Think in terms of keywords, always asking yourself how you are going to find this file when you want it. If the client's name is Freiholtz, but you can never spell it right and, anyway, you always think of that project as the McMansion, name the file McMansion (unless others will see it). If you keep track of your family's vaccinations, illnesses, and hospitalizations, the names of the folder and its files are simple:

Health

  Charles

  Bess

  Maggie

  Sam

  General (or Notes)

In the last file, you can note items about flu symptoms, cardiofitness routines, and other information you might someday want. When you call up a file, you'll type "health\maggie".

It's possible to use long file names, but you're better off keeping them short and descriptive. They're easier to use and won't baffle some programs.

If you receive an error message when naming a file, you may have used a reserved character, such as $<, >, :, ", /, \, ?, *,$ or $|$. Also, don't use spaces in file names—although they are allowed in some software, some operating systems don't recognize them, so it's safer to avoid them. And because some software is case-sensitive, it's easier to use all lowercase letters in file names so that you don't have to remember who uses what.

An extension (a period and three letters, for example, .doc or .rtf) usually follows a file name, but this is added automatically.

File naming can get very sophisticated, especially in companies where teams work on a number of different projects. In that case, be a sheep; follow the group system.

▶ *Deleting files.* When in doubt, don't. If you can't decide whether you'll need that information again, put it in storage. When housecleaning, if you find files that relate to someone else, forward them to that person. Never delete program (software) files if you aren't very sure of what you're doing. If you use temporary files (.tmp), use that extension only for truly temporary material (kept for a matter of a day at most), and then regularly delete all .tmp files.

▶ *Housecleaning.* Reading about setting up files properly is all well and good. The hard part is making sense of what you've already got on your computer. With the outline form firmly in your head, scroll down your main folders and open each one.

- Ask yourself whether the items in this folder make sense

- Ask yourself whether each file belongs in this category. If not, drag the misfiled files to the correct folder.

- Delete unnecessary or temporary files.

- Check similar file names to see if the material duplicates or is a revised version of an earlier file. Unless you need earlier versions, keep the latest and delete earlier versions and duplicate material.

It sounds tedious, but if you devote 10 minutes here and 15 minutes there to this type of housecleaning, anything you need will be right where you expect it to be.

Today's pack rats are hoarding gigabytes of data and finding that pressing "delete" is just as hard as tossing old belongings in the trash.
—MARK MCCLUSKEY (2007)

▶ *Desktop.* If your desktop is crammed with icons and you're always bent over peering to find the one you need, it's time to clear it off. Reserve your desktop for the handful of icons (including a shortcut to the documents you are currently working on) that you use most often, and keep these on the toolbar. Yes, it's easy to stash things on the desktop, but as soon as you've viewed them, park them where they belong. Installing new programs can leave you with shortcut icons on the screen. Windows has a desktop "cleaning wizard" that automatically takes care of some of this, but you might want to disable the wizard and do a manual cleaning so that you know what you've got and what went where.

Maintenance

For a long time, I let the huge amount of computer-operation information intimidate me. Then, I realized I didn't know how my phone worked, either. But I knew how to make phone calls.

—SALLY WILLIAMS (1989)

Most of us know how to use computers, although we don't know much about them. You can still, however, do some simple maintenance jobs that will keep your computer working more efficiently and save you time lost in having it lock up or otherwise misbehave.

▶ A number of products for keeping your screen clean are available. Turn the screen off while you clean it. The first time you use a product, test it in whatever corner of the screen you use least and wait to see if it affects the screen adversely. And wipe, don't rub, your screen.

▶ Dust the outside of your electronic equipment with a damp cloth, and turn the keyboard upside down now and then and shake it out. Dust can clog your fan airflow and overheat your CPU. A can of compressed air will chase away most of the dust. If you're comfortable doing it, you can take the case off your computer (after unplugging it and grounding yourself so you don't cause any static electricity) and dust inside with the compressed air.

- If you have a PC, run "disk cleanup" regularly. This utility frees up space on your hard drive by finding and deleting (if you say so) files that you don't need—for example, temporary files and Internet files. It also empties your recycle bin.

- Defragment your hard drive regularly, depending on what kind of computer work you do and how much. Information gets laid down on your hard drive randomly. When your computer has to hunt here and there for bits and pieces of what you're working on, it takes longer. Defragmenting reassembles your data in a logical, linear format. Some people might defragment once a year if they're doing nothing but word processing. Others might want to defragment once a week or once a month. If you don't have your disk defragmenter on your "start" menu, set up a shortcut to make it quick and easy for yourself. Shut down all running programs and run the disk cleanup before defragmenting. If you have a large, full drive, defragmenting could take hours, so start it as you're leaving for the day.

- When you start a new project, this is a good time to clean up the old projects. Scroll through your directories to see which folders and their files can be moved to storage, which can be deleted altogether, and which are misfiled.

- At the same time, look at your list of bookmarked sites (Favorites on Internet Explorer, for example). If you haven't checked them for a while, you'll find duplicates, links that don't work, information you're no longer interested in, and some sites in the wrong categories.

Tips

- When you experience problems with your computer, turn it off and back on again. According to Aaron Schildkraut (www.myhometech.net), "Nine times out of ten, rebooting your computer—and any equipment that connects to it—will solve the problem."

- In fact, turning off your computer overnight or when it's not in use not only saves energy but clears out the RAM (temporary memory), which otherwise would slow your machine down over time.

- If you use your laptop on a public Wi-Fi system, don't forget that even when you use an encrypted (and thus supposedly safe) system, nearby hackers can capture your passwords.

- Few of us exploit the full capabilities of our software (statistics indicate that we use only 15 percent of our software features). The next time you have 10 minutes between appointments, pick up the manual for some of your software and check the index for an unfamiliar term. Look it up and expand your knowledge of that software. It might be something that you can use.

- One of the most consistent time-savers your computer offers is the keystroke macro, where you program one key plus alt (in some programs) to produce a word, phrase, sentence, or paragraph (even an entire letter) that you use over and over again. Suppose you write many letters saying essentially, "Thank you for your submission. Although another house might be interested, it is not something that we see ourselves publishing at this time." You can add sentences before or after or in between, but it's a big help to be able to hit a key plus alt, and bingo, there's a paragraph that you don't have to type again.

- Because you can file the same document in as many folders as you want to, you can either duplicate the document so that it's wherever you need it or create shortcuts from various places to its one central location. Since most hard drives will never be filled, duplication of material is a problem only if you do a lot of this and all the duplicates are clogging active files.

- Depending on the type of files and how useful it is to see a chronology, include the date in file names: tokyo2008, jackson090108, jackson101108, empire9nov09.

- Make sure your work setup is as convenient and comfortable as possible. Would a display stand (to raise your monitor), a different computer drawer, or an ergonomic chair make a difference? Play with the elements you have and look for maximum comfort, posture help, and flexibility.

- Create a new file even before you have very much information about a project or topic. Louise Erdrich wrote once that she thought "a title is like a magnet. It begins to draw these scraps of experience or conversation or memory to it. Eventually, it collects a book." In the same way, if you open a file called Memories or Movies or Restaurants, it'll make it easy for you to drop in anecdotes you think of, names of movies you want to see, or restaurants to which you can take visitors. When you are working on a project, opening files on various aspects of it will either collect information under that heading or wither away for lack of it.

▶ As many as one of every ten laptops will be stolen during its lifetime. To protect yours, consider buying a cable lock, which you use to attach the laptop to a table leg or heavy chair in cafés, hotels, workshops, airports, or other public places where you might take your eye off it just long enough for someone to pick it up. Tracing programs exist, but they involve money and some loss of privacy. But do look into them—they might work for you. Engraving your name and business phone number on your laptop may be a deterrent, as it then cannot be sold. You might also set up a system password, so that when someone tries to turn your computer on, absolutely nothing happens without the password. Travel with your laptop in an inconspicuous carrier, something that looks more like a large purse, briefcase, or backpack than a computer case.

▶ If you are subject to electrical outages, consider a battery backup that would allow you to work right through a short or medium-length loss of electricity.

The mind can store an estimated 100 trillion bits of information—compared with which a computer's mere billions are virtually amnesiac.
—Sharon Begley (1986)

▶ On bad computer days, remember that you're better than a computer any old time.

Organizing Aids

▶ *CD/DVD holders.* You can keep each written CD/DVD in a plastic sleeve or box, but you can store more of them more conveniently, and in less space, by using an album-type book with slotted pages. Keep a marking pen in, on, or next to the book so that you never forget to label a disk.

▶ *Cordless keyboard and mouse.* If you haven't gone cordless with your desktop keyboard and mouse, you might consider it. When you're organizing files, you'll feel more friendly toward the task if you can put your feet up on your desk and work at deleting and moving and housecleaning in a comfortable position.

▶ *Flash drive (travel drive).* If you don't have one, you probably need one. Nothing is so convenient for transferring data from one computer to another, for an instant quick backup, and to let you carry data with you in the smallest possible form.

▶ *Software.* If you love your computer and make the most of it, looking at software is like being a kid in a candy store again. Almost anything you could want ("Oh, if only I had . . ."), someone has already developed software for. You've probably already found your own games, genealogy, and greeting-card software, but you might want to look into organizing software. For some people, it adds extra, somewhat complicated steps to their life. Others take to it like ducks to water. These packages usually come with a calendar, appointment book, To Do list, address book, alarms, and other refinements you haven't thought of yet. In addition to dedicated organizing software, there's software that helps you manage specific areas of your life: finances, paper management, inventory, taxes, scheduling, productivity, or bookkeeping.

CHAPTER 12

How to Organize Your Personal Life

> *The simple idea that everyone needs a*
> *reasonable amount of challenging work in his*
> *or her life, and also a personal life, complete*
> *with noncompetitive leisure, has never really*
> *taken hold.*
>
> —JUDITH MARTIN (1985)

Joan Collins once said, "The secret of having a personal life is not answering too many questions about it." There are other secrets to having a personal life outside the needs of family, work, and community contributions. Some of them you need to discover for yourself. Other shortcuts and suggestions are included here.

The People in Your Life

In an ideal world, your social life is fashioned by you, in accordance with your own likes and pleasures. However, life is rarely so tidy. See Chapter 5, "Dealing with People," for ways to manage the way other people relate to *you*. This section deals with organizing yourself as you relate to *others*.

Tips

▶ Remembering birthdays, anniversaries, graduations, and other happenings in the lives of family and friends:

- Make a chronological list of birthdays and anniversaries (wedding, death, sobriety), including years, so that if it's a landmark (twenty-first birthday or fiftieth wedding anniversary), you'll realize it. If you keep this list on your computer, you can highlight and copy those occurring this month to your To Do list for the month.

- Buy greeting cards in bulk. If you choose carefully, you can come away from a dollar store with a nice assortment of cards that you'll be proud to send. One woman with a large family who lives an hour from the nearest store has an entire bottom drawer dedicated to cards separated by labeled pieces of cardboard: Hanukkah, Valentine's Day, Get Well, Thank You, Birthdays, Congratulations, and so on. Keep resupplying yourself and you'll never be faced with either ignoring an important event or making a special trip to the store for a card.

- On the first day of the month, choose and address cards for all those you want to remember this month. In the upper right-hand corner, indicate the date of the event (7/21). Place the cards in chronological order. A few days before each event, add a note to the card, stamp it right over your penciled date, and mail it. Having the cards already addressed and knowing the date they're due is more than half the battle.

- In the case of a thank-you note, address a notecard as soon as you think of it. Add a stamp, and it's so ready to go that you're quite likely to dash off the thank-you note instead of living with nagging guilt and discomfort about an unsent "thank you."

- You'll find some very effective birthday-reminder sites online. You spend a few minutes filling in—just once!—birth dates and anniversaries. After that, you receive an e-mail saying, for example, "It's one week until Jerry's birthday."

- You'll save time if you keep postage stamps, a small scale, and the bookmarked site of the U.S. Postal Service on hand. In seconds you can weigh your card to make sure it's only one ounce, thus taking one stamp. If it's over one ounce, look up the correct postage on the USPS Postage Price Calculator site (www.postcalc.usps.gov). No waiting in line at the post office for you.

- Online greeting card sites can be too much hill, but many of them have cards that can be personalized and sent free; for higher quality e-cards, you might pay an annual fee for all your cards. Some of the singing, action cards are delightful—however, for some people, the pleasure still doesn't equal that of a snail-mail card with a personal note.

▶ Gift giving is a personal choice. A good case can be made for limiting gift giving to only the most important occasions. Most of us already have too much stuff, and few of us know what another person already has, doesn't need, or doesn't like, making it difficult to find the right gift.

- In most cases, the best gifts are consumable; that is, they can be used up, leaving nothing that needs shelf room: scented, soy, or long-burning candles; jams or relishes; homemade cookies or fudge; a selection of household tapes (duct, electrician, masking, double-sided, cellophane); wine or fancy liqueurs; stationery or notecards; a sheet of commemorative postage stamps; movie tickets; single magazines (probably not subscriptions, in case the person doesn't like it well enough to have it coming in every month); used books; gift certificates; candies; colorful paper plates, cups, and napkins; handmade coupons good for babysitting or housecleaning; an outing to a playground for a child, to the theater for an adult, or to the zoo for anyone.

- Take someone close to you to lunch, followed by a stop at a sporting goods store or a department store. Help them choose a gift that you pay for. The gift will be something that they truly want, and you'll both have enjoyed the gift of time together.

- Dedicate a cupboard, closet shelf, large box, or other space to gift materials: wrapping paper, scissors, ribbons, cellophane tape, tags, bows, and gifts you buy in anticipation of an event. Keep a few general-purpose gifts on hand for unexpected occasions: candles, attractive decks of cards, an inexpensive domino game, a bottle or two of wine.

- Many yard sales have straw baskets for a quarter. With a bow on the handle, they're an inexpensive, attractive, and reusable "wrapping" for a gift.

- Online shopping makes gift giving easy: gift certificates to major sites, like Amazon.com or eBay, are appreciated by most computer users, and online gift registries for wedding and baby gifts allow you to be thoughtful in just minutes. You can order flowers, fresh fruit, or baskets of gifts that you choose yourself. Almost anything you can conceive of can be found somewhere online. For example, one site, www.caregifting.com, specializes in gifts that are of practical use to the sick or grieving.

- Depending on how important gift giving is to you, you might keep a computer or notebook list of gift ideas. If you find that your boss is a fervent golfer, you have a clue for a gift; write it down. While driving to work, you may think of the perfect gift for someone; make a note of it before you forget it. When you see something clever and think what a great gift it would make, write it down. You'll thank yourself when you're scrambling for ideas for a last-minute gift.

▶ Caregiving may become a part of your life for a week or a month or even years when someone close to you is very ill or dying. A great deal is involved in this, including watching out for your own mental and physical well-being. To survive this time gracefully, develop a plan for dealing with what needs to be dealt with. As is often the case, start online, where you will find information and even practical help. For example, www.lotsahelpinghands.com helps you coordinate caregivers.

Organizing Aids

▶ Box, shelf, or drawer to hold greeting cards and notepaper

▶ Gifts for unexpected occasions

▶ List of important birthdays and anniversaries

▶ Selection of greeting cards

▶ Wrapping paper, scissors, ribbons, cellophane tape, tags, and bows

Reading

Reading is included here because even if you're reading work materials, you're not likely to be spending much time with your feet up on your desk reading while you're at work. Most people catch up on their reading after hours.

If you are fortunate enough to have a spare corner in your living room or bedroom, make yourself a reading nook. All you need is a comfortable chair (either a recliner or a chair with an ottoman), good lighting, a lightweight throw, and a tabletop on which to put your extra reading and your evening beverage. When space is tight, install a wall sconce for light and a wall-mounted magazine rack.

Tips

▶ Speed reading isn't just reading fast, it's reading smart. When you're reading for information rather than for pleasure, you can absorb the main ideas of a book by reading the book jacket first to get the overall picture, then the table of contents to see what issues the book deals with. Skim the chapters that interest you, reading the subject headings, the first and last paragraphs under each, and the chapter conclusion. Sometimes you will want to read every word of a book, but when you have a stack of books to read to see "what's out there," this kind of selective reading will give you a working overview.

▶ When you put a journal or magazine in your "to read" pile, always put it on the bottom of the pile or at the back of the rack so that the publications will be in chronological order when you have time to catch up.

▶ Nothing should go in your reading pile that must be read by a certain date. Keep those items separate, with the date to be read by marked on a sticky-back note.

▶ Don't let catalogs pile up—they'll just make your reading pile look worse than it is—and read each one only once. At that time, tear out pages with items you're interested in and staple them to the ripped-off front cover (where there might be a discount coupon code) and back cover (you'll need your customer number for ordering).

- If you read a number of professional journals or niche magazines, tear out and staple together those articles that you want to read. You can then keep an article or two in your briefcase for reading while you're waiting for a meeting or an appointment.

- Team reading is a big help if you're in a profession that has to keep up with the latest information (that's probably all professions). Parcel out reports, journals, books, and articles to members of the team. Each e-mails the others with a summary of key information.

- Cut back on the amount of reading that comes your way by canceling subscriptions to magazines and journals that aren't truly important or necessary to you. Go to www.catalogchoice.com to get your name off catalog mailing lists (you unsubscribe by individual catalog, which allows you to get rid of the cat and dog catalogs because you have neither but keep your much-treasured cookware catalogs).

- Keeping up with the news could take all day if you let it. Television is probably the least efficient way to get the news, as much of the time is spent on insignificant or packaged-for-entertainment pieces. You can subscribe online to a number of news services that will speedily give you the news highlights, leaving it to you to pursue the stories you need to know more about. If you want to know what has been in the news during the past week, a weekly newsmagazine sums it up nicely, and although they somewhat resemble television news, you at least have the option of turning the page if something doesn't interest you.

- Post-it flags are a reader's best friend. These repositionable sticky flags come in various colors and sizes and allow you to mark places in an article or book that you want to go back to, copy, pass on, or otherwise make note of.

- Small, battery-powered reading lamps are useful if your bed partner falls asleep earlier than you do, on camping trips, on an overseas flight, while driving at night (no, you're not the driver), or when sleeping on someone's floor or couch.

Just the knowledge that a good book is awaiting one at the end of a long day makes that day happier.

—Kathleen Norris (1931)

- Keep a reading list of titles, authors, and subjects that interest you, and get most of your books from a library.

- If you own thousands of books, you have no doubt already figured out a way to organize them or you are beyond help. If you have hundreds, consider keeping them all in the same room and making a wall of bookshelves. This takes less actual and less visual space than having several sets of bookshelves around the house. Organize them by topics and, within topics, alphabetically. Organizing by size and color, although it looks nice, makes people think you don't really read.

- Most book clubs choose one book that everyone reads and then discusses at the next gathering. In today's information-rich world, with over 170,000 books published every year in the United States, you might enjoy it more if each person reads and reports on a different book. You'll either hear about a book that you want to read or hear enough to let you almost feel that you've read the book yourself.

Organizing Aids

- Bookmarks
- Bookshelves
- Magazine rack
- Personal reading light
- Post-it flags

Finances

Being organized, keeping careful records, and planning ahead are rarely as important as they are in your financial life. Most of us feel like the anonymous woman who said, "I have enough money to last me the rest of my life, unless I buy something." And, oddly enough, it

There are a handful of people whom money won't spoil, and we all count ourselves among them.

—MIGNON MCLAUGHLIN
(1966)

hardly matters what a person earns; the majority of us are living out at the financial edges of our incomes. You can do a few things about that.

Tips

▶ Keep all bills, credit card receipts, and money matters in one well-defined spot. Most of the average family's money paper would fit in a 9×12×4″ box. Take care of money at the same place at least once a month. You probably need to write checks for bills more often than once a month because the grace period on most bills has shrunk considerably; nobody gets a month's grace anymore.

▶ Have a system for paying all bills on time. Make it a matter of pride that you never pay finance charges. Keep bills in a special holder, with the date due written in the upper-right-hand corner of each envelope (which you'll cover with a stamp), and every day look to see which ones need to be mailed. Be generous with your estimate of delivery time. Credit card companies aren't interested in what you think of the post office's delivery habits.

▶ Keep an envelope or box handy so that everyone in the house puts in their credit card receipts, bank-deposit slips, and ATM-withdrawal slips. If you share accounts, one person must ultimately be responsible for keeping the checkbook balanced and the bills paid. If that doesn't work, you need separate accounts.

> *People keep telling us about their love affairs, when what we really want to know is how much money they make and how they manage on it.*
> —MIGNON MCLAUGHLIN
> (1963)

▶ To draw up a budget, make four lists:

1. List of monthly fixed payouts: rent or mortgage, utilities, basic telephone service, cell phone basic charge, loan payments, day care, tuition, cable TV. Any fixed amount that has to be paid every month goes here.

2. List of fixed annual expenses: property taxes, homeowner's or renter's insurance, homeowner's assessments, car insurance, umbrella insurance. Anything you pay once a year goes here.

3. List of monthly necessities that vary, so you must estimate how much you spend on them each month: food, medical copays, transportation, clothing.

4. List of monthly expenses that aren't strictly necessary but that you tend to see on your credit cards or in your checkbook: eating out, liquor, book purchases, entertaining, babysitters, movie rentals.

Your lists will be tailored to your life and will be much more precise, but the four categories are key. Add up List 2, divide the total by 12, and add that sum to List 1. Be realistic about your estimates of the items on List 3, add them up, and add that figure to List 1. Subtract the total of List 1 from your net monthly income, and you see how much disposable income you have each month. That is what you have available to spend on List 4.

▶ Drawing up a budget and discussing it with anyone who shares financial responsibility with you is important because, for example, a significant percentage of people today can't tell you how 25 percent of their income is spent. Other thought-provoking figures (which vary with the source and date of research): 59 percent of Americans have credit card debt, about 40 percent of supermarket purchases are impulse buys, women's clothing buys are 49 percent impulse purchases, and possibly as much as 60 percent of all shopping decisions are made in the store. It's very hard to save and stay out of debt with so many unknowns in the budget. Try to corral some of those figures and be conscious of impulse buys; stick to your lists.

▶ Simplify your life by (1) having your salary deposited directly into your checking account, (2) having an amount taken automatically from your checking account every month and deposited in your savings account, (3) having some regular bills of predictable amounts (your mortgage or rent, for example) paid automatically, and (4) paying as many bills as possible online. This will save you time, stamps, and worrying about late payments.

- ▶ Many excellent Web sites explain exactly how to balance your checkbook. It ought to be balanced every month, and all parties with an interest in that account should review the month's spending.

Organizing Aids

- ▶ Paper trays
- ▶ Letter holder

Automobile

> *A car is just a moving, giant handbag! You never have actually to carry groceries, or dry cleaning, or anything! You can have five pairs of shoes with you at all times!*
> —CYNTHIA HEIMEL (1993)

If you've ever seen the inside of a giant handbag, you do not want your car to look like one. You'll feel much better about yourself if you get into a tidy car; some people think that you'll even drive better. It takes very little to keep a car clean, but it takes a lot of time and effort to shovel out one that would be an archaeologist-analyst's dream.

Always look behind you when you leave the car, and take with you anything that doesn't belong there.

Tips

- ▶ Your very first move after purchasing an automobile should be to make copies of the keys. This is one purchase that you'll never regret. If you have never mislaid or lost your car keys, you can skip this. For everyone else, stash duplicate keys in safe but accessible places. The old magnetized key holder is a possibility; affix it to the unlikeliest spot on the underside of the car. Give one to a neighbor or good friend whose phone number you know by heart. Keep one in your desk drawer. If more than one person uses this car, you'll want a key on the keyrack by the house door in addition to each driver having their own key—each one with a color-coded holder so that you can tell whose keys are lost and whose are found. If you ever get locked out of your car, it will be at absolutely the most inconvenient time in your life.

▶ File all your auto records: title, registration tags, insurance, maintenance receipts, accidents, and repairs.

▶ Unless you have mechanical skills that include knowledge of how cars are computerized today, you need to rely on a professional. What you can take care of yourself, however, will save you money and, surprisingly, even time:

• Change the oil as recommended for your vehicle (if you don't know, do it every 3,000 miles). You can do this yourself (see www.doityourself.com) or have it done. The advantage of having it done is that in addition to the oil change, the service provider will generally replace the oil filter, check fluid levels, and, at your request, rotate your tires.

• Change air filters at least once a year (or more often, if recommended for your vehicle). Keeping clean filters in your car will improve its performance. See how to do it at www.edmunds.com.

• Rotate your tires every 4,000 to 5,000 miles. You can do this yourself, although you need to know what you're doing. However, it's not that expensive to have your tires rotated with a tune-up or lube job.

• Take your car in for a tune-up ("major service") approximately every two years or 30,000 miles. Before you go in, print out a list of recommended replacements (see www.ehow.com) so that you can compare it with your bill.

• Once a year, give your car (or pay for) a thorough cleaning inside and out, including shampooing or otherwise cleaning the upholstery. In between times, keep it washed and waxed (every 90 days is recommended for waxing), and shop-vac or hand-vac the interior. Naturally, you should remove trash and detritus as they accumulate.

▶ If your car needs repairs, check with www.repairpal.com before you go in for a comprehensive explanation of what typical repairs should cost based on the make, model, and year of the car and your ZIP code.

- Glove compartment basics include ownership papers, a current insurance card, a change pouch or coin holder with quarters for meters, inexpensive all-purpose sunglasses that can be used whether you wear eyeglasses or not, a small flashlight, pen and paper, a list of emergency phone numbers, hard candy, and tissues. You may also want to keep a few moistened towelettes, napkins, rolled-up plastic bags for trash, and a portable umbrella.

- Automobile organizer–type accessories have multiplied: portable "offices," compartmented bags that hang over a seat and hold small items, notepads that can be attached to the dashboard, map readers that combine magnification with a light, E-ZPass holders, visor organizers, drink holders, trunk organizers, and tote organizers so that you can stash bags in them and then carry them into the house all together. Keep your maps in one of the door compartments, which are just the right size for most of them and will keep them from getting wrinkled.

- A hard-to-resist "must have" for the automobile is the escape hammer. Pointed solid steel heads at either end can be used to break side windows in case your car goes into a river or your electrical system fails in an emergency situation. A razor-sharp (but protected) blade can cut through jammed seatbelts. In addition, the hammer features a flashing red light and a bright beam. It's difficult to know if we could remember to keep this handy enough to use it in an emergency, and how lifesaving it really might be. On the other hand, it would, at the very least, make a great gift for someone.

Organizing Aids

- Coin holder
- Compartmented organizers
- Escape hammer
- Flashlight
- Map reader
- Notepaper and pencil

Wardrobe

For help with organizing your closets, drawers, and other storage places for your wardrobe and accessories, see Chapter 8.

First, ask yourself if you need to "organize" your wardrobe. If you have little or no trouble laying your hands on the right clothes for your life, you haven't got a problem, even if a stranger looks into your closet and gasps, "What happened here?"

If, however, you lose time every day trying to match tops to bottoms or shoes to suits, if you often end up uncomfortable in public because you don't feel right in what you're wearing, or if the clothes part of your life irritates you, you probably should organize your wardrobe.

Any garment that makes you feel bad will make you look bad.
—VICTORIA BILLINGS (1974)

Tips

▶ Do not buy new clothing until you have thoroughly organized your old clothing because you won't yet know precisely what pieces will fill which gaps.

▶ If you live in an area with seasons, your first sorting is by spring/summer and fall/winter. If you have an extra closet in your house, it's convenient to store your off-season clothes there (making sure that all of them are clean, repaired, and ready to go). If not, keep them in the least-used part of your closet in clothes bags, which means that they stay clean and you don't have to look at them.

▶ Next, sort the clothes you are wearing now by type (shirts, blouses, slacks, dresses, suits, jackets, two-piece outfits) and then, within categories, by color.

You mean those clothes of hers are intentional? My heavens, I always thought she was on her way out of a burning building.
—DOROTHY PARKER (1942)

▶ Examine each article of clothing and ask: have I worn this in the last year? If not, try to imagine under what circumstances you would wear it. If you can't imagine any, it goes in the discard pile on the bed no matter how much you like it. If you do wear it, what do you wear it with? If it's a shirt, what suit or what slacks? If it's a blouse, what skirt or what suit? If you do not find something that's a great match for the item, decide whether to keep it and purchase something to go with it, or whether it's not worth the expense and should go in the discard pile. Do this for all your clothes until everything left in the closet works for you. By now you'll also have a list of purchases that will round out your wardrobe.

▶ Examine your shoes carefully, discarding those that are not a great fit and those that you never wear. Don't keep shoes that don't go with anything else.

▶ Do the same thing for your underwear, sleepwear, robes, sports clothes, and swimwear. If you tackle one category a week, you'll have a great wardrobe by the time you have to switch this group to the off-season. Just kidding.

▶ Also considered part of your wardrobe are outerwear, jackets and sweaters, shawls and wraps, gloves, scarves, hats, and jewelry.

▶ The goal in looking at your wardrobe is to simplify (keep fewer items) and maximize (one skirt can support four different tops).

▶ As you go, check all clothing for needed repairs or upkeep. Having something in your closet that is in no shape to wear is not really having something in your closet.

▶ Clothes that you seldom wear should be boxed up and stored either under the bed or on the top closet shelf.

▶ Avoid clothes that need drycleaning or need to be laundered after each wearing.

▶ Wardrobes are a great deal more complex than this, but if you get this far, you won't have any trouble finding something to wear tomorrow.

Organizing Aids

▶ Clothing bags

▶ Nonslip pants hangers

- ▶ Padded hangers
- ▶ Shoe racks
- ▶ Storage boxes
- ▶ Suit hangers
- ▶ Tie racks

Briefcases, Purses, Wallets, and Carryalls

Our briefcases, purses, and wallets generally contain irreplaceable material. Losing one is usually fairly disastrous. Make sure it's a small disaster by (1) being very conscious of where these items are at all times when you're in public, (2) carrying the minimum necessary, and (3) making copies of any documents in them.

> *The lost wallet or purse law: No matter how careful you are, assume that you will lose a few. . . . Keep grief to a minimum. It's bad enough your stuff is gone; don't lose your mind too.*
> —JENNIFER JAMES (1993)

Tips

- ▶ *Briefcase.* Always keep in it (perhaps in a small case) the office supplies you need most often when you're away from your desk: pens, scissors, cellophane tape, paperclips, a small stapler, sticky-back notes, a few postage stamps. In a folder, to protect them, carry a few sheets of letterhead stationery, envelopes, personal-size stationery, memo paper, and blank paper. Add whatever you need for comfort: tissues, mints, a granola bar. These items are permanent residents of your briefcase. Whenever you leave your office, you add whatever is necessary for your next few hours plus an article from your reading pile in case you get stuck somewhere. Keep your briefcase near your desk at work so that you can drop things into it as you come across them, and by the door at home so that you can pick it up on your way out.

- ▶ *Wallet or billfold.* Your driver's license is the key item here, although a credit card runs a close second. To lessen hassles in case of theft, take only one credit card with you except when you know you'll be using others. Photocopy everything in your billfold front and back, and keep the copies in a safe place. Not only is this incredibly useful if your wallet is stolen, but it is a superstitious protection ensuring that it never is; it's only the people who wish they had photocopied everything whose wallets get stolen. When you add a new card or have your driver's license renewed, don't forget to photocopy it and add it to your file. Be sure your billfold or wallet contains important emergency information: your physician's name and phone number, your next of kin and phone number, and your blood type, along with any critical medical information (you wear a defibrillator; you take a blood thinner; you are allergic to penicillin).

▶ *Purse.* Evening bags are too small to need organizing, but the daytime purse that goes to work can easily resemble a piece of carry-on luggage. The biggest advantage of these purses is that they can hold everything. The biggest disadvantage is that you can't find anything in them. Invest in a set of small travel bags in different colors: the red one holds all your pens, papers, and paperclips; the blue one has all your makeup; the green one has all those odd things that gravitate to the bottom of the purse: Band-Aids, mints, moist towelettes, fingernail file, your Red Cross knife, lip balm. The items will vary, but choose three categories; you'll be able to identify each just by looking in your purse. Keys sink to the bottom, travel from purse compartment to purse compartment and, in short, are usually the last item that you pull out. Attach some identifying object to your key ring— something that can be felt and seen easily: a bright-colored, small stuffed animal; a tape measure on a ring, which can also come in handy; a bright yellow rubber chicken; a fluorescent rubber spike ball—some of these light up when you squeeze them, and you can't mistake their feel. Alternatively, attach your key ring to a clip on the outside of your purse where it's always visible.

▶ *Carryall.* A large, sturdy bag with handles has dozens of uses for hauling things from home to work and back again, and everywhere else as well. Like your briefcase, park this at the door at home and at your office so that you can drop things into it as you think of them; the bag is ready to go when you are.

Hobbies

No one can give you a hobby. Falling in love with woodcarving or photography or quilting or spelunking or scrapbooking or building model trains or collecting coins or making jewelry is a mixture of chemistry, opportunity, and energy.

> *Leisure and the cultivation of human capacities are inextricably interdependent.*
> —MARGARET MEAD (1963)

However, most hobbies will benefit from a little organizing: first, to keep them from taking over the entire house, and second, to keep them from becoming such a mess that you begin to lose interest.

Hobby organizing uses the same principles as anything else:

► Dedicate one place as your workplace; don't let your materials stray from there, and don't allow in any items that don't belong.

► Set up a flat workspace if you need one; if space is limited, a corner table or desk helps, especially if you use the wall space above it for storage.

► Be your own best friend: leave things neat for yourself so that you don't dread getting back to it, and choose a breaking point just when things are getting interesting so that you'll be eager to return to it.

► Break up your hobby materials into parts (like with like): books, tools, finished sections, in-progress sections, materials, and so on.

► Schedule similar tasks for one time: do as much of the gluing, or sanding, or cutting as you can.

► After you're familiar with your materials, gather or buy containers that suit them: boxes, bins, or nail and screw organizing cabinets for small items, pegboard if you have lots of tools to hang, baskets, rolling storage carts, stacked drawers, or Stanton carts (see Chapter 9).

Tips

▶ If you are a collector, you need a good way to display your miners' headlamps, inkwells, geodes, Occupied Japan figurines, silver mustard pots, miniature tea sets, rhinestone jewelry, or antique tools. You're the best judge of what will show them off to their advantage and for your pleasure, but two very nice words are "behind glass." Display cabinets or cases are available in every material, color, size, and shape. They will keep your collection in one place, you won't need to dust them very often, and people won't be so tempted to handle them.

▶ One "hobby" that we seldom think of as such but that conforms to many of the definitions of a hobby is our collection of photographs. Luckily for those of you who were born into the digital age, there is software for every possible photo-organizing need. Even you, however, may get handed a box of family photos to organize.

- If you're just getting started, set yourself up with durable, matching photo albums for which you can buy pages for every kind of photo: $8^1/_2 \times 11''$ to the ancient $3 \times 3''$. For odd-sized photos, buy pages on which you can make a collage.

- Find a place to work where you can leave your materials out for days or even weeks. It's no fun to have to lay everything out and sort it again.

- For either digital or film photos, get into the habit very early on of tossing bad photos. We hate to do this because somehow it feels as though we're tossing away the person in the photo. It's easy to delete or discard blurry photos, but the purely bad ones are more difficult. Try. You will never miss them. If you're really in a quandary, put all questionable photos in a folder to look at next time you're working on the photos. By then you may realize that you can discard them.

- If you're sorting hundreds of photos, make up manila envelopes for people who you think might like some of your duplicates or near-duplicates. After 30 years, you have had plenty of time to enjoy photos of your nieces and nephews; the time has come to return those photos to their parents for distribution to the n's and n's.

- You'll have to make a decision about identifying photos: names, dates, and anything else that's pertinent. One way is to jot notes on the back of each photograph. Don't use a fountain pen, which may stain the photo, or a ballpoint, which will emboss it. Pencil is all right if you don't press very hard, but it may smudge. Buy a special photo marking pencil or a film marking pen. You can also put a legend on a sticky-back note and attach it to the back of the photo. As long as the photo is in an album, the note won't get dislodged. In both these cases, you can read the information only by taking the photo out of the album and turning it over. The third way is to type the legend and glue it under the photo or handprint it under the photo so that it can be read while looking at the photo. Some albums include white space for this purpose.

- Many people hesitate to take a scissors to a photo—it feels like scribbling in a book or something that you oughtn't to do. We crop digital photos; why not paper photos? You'll like many pictures in your album much better if you trim them.

- Sort your photos by individual, by year, or by events. But do remember that just getting them into albums is a major accomplishment. If you have to skimp on one phase of this job, skimp on the organizing part. As long as they are labeled so that people can figure out who's who, you should accept a big pat on the back just for getting the photos out of boxes and drawers and cracks in the floor and old luggage and into nice albums.

- As you're sorting, think ahead to birthday and holiday gifts. Set aside any great photos that could be made into postcards, T-shirts, posters, puzzles, or even postage stamps that can actually be used.

- With the proper equipment and enough time, you can scan all your old photographs into your computer and then manipulate them digitally. This will preserve them for much longer, and they won't take up space. It's a big job, but the results are rewarding.

- To keep up with your photos during the year, dedicate a box to photos and toss in everything that comes your way. At the end of the year, you can put a lid on the box, mark it with the year, and store it, or you can put the photos into albums while you watch a movie some night.

- Some people save negatives. No one can stop you from doing so, but this is possibly one of those situations in which 99 percent of negatives are never needed again. For the 1 percent that might be—only "might," mind you—one wonders if it's worth the trouble of keeping them. If you must, at least put the year on each batch.

Organizing Aids

- ▶ Baskets, bins, boxes, and drawers
- ▶ Display cabinets
- ▶ Flat working surface
- ▶ Photo albums
- ▶ Rolling storage carts
- ▶ Stanton carts

Travel

A trip is what you take when you can't take any more of what you've been taking.
—ADELINE AINSWORTH (1973)

You may be traveling for business, but it still affects your personal life. Both personal travel and business travel require you to plan ahead.

Tips

- ▶ Question the necessity of every business trip. If your position requires you to travel, you haven't a choice, but the financial, physical, and mental costs of traveling today mean that you don't travel without a good reason. Some business can be carried out effectively by computer, phone, teleconferencing, videoconferencing, and plain old paper. You might also look carefully at pleasure trips. Once you select a destination, everything else follows and you may be on the verge of departure before it dawns on you that you'd rather be going somewhere else.

▶ Keep a packing list on your computer that contains everything you could possibly need on a trip. Copy that list into your notes for your upcoming trip, and all you have to do is delete the trenchcoat, dress shoes, and sweater that you won't need for Cancún. The following is a sample list; most of the things on it are unnecessary for most trips, but having one overarching list keeps you from forgetting anything.

- Adapters/converters
- Addresses
- Airline tickets or e-tickets
- Alarm clock
- Aspirin or acetaminophen
- Baggies
- Band-Aids
- Bathrobe
- Beach towel
- Billfold
- Binoculars or opera glasses
- Briefcase
- Business cards
- Caftan
- Calculator
- Camera, spare batteries
- Car and hotel reservations information
- Carry-on
- Cell phone, iPod, BlackBerry
- Checkbook
- Cosmetic bag

- Credit cards
- Deck of cards
- Deodorant
- Destination notes
- Driver's license
- Electric shaver
- Eyeglasses or reading glasses
- Fanny pack
- Flashlight
- Gifts
- Gloves
- Guidebooks and maps
- Hair dryer and hair-care accessories
- Hard candy
- Insect repellant
- International Driver's License
- Itinerary
- Jacket
- Kleenex, moist towelettes, toilet tissue
- Laundry detergent and clothesline
- Luggage
- Makeup
- Medications
- Money belt
- Money—U.S. and foreign
- Notebook computer
- Notebook and pens
- Oral antibiotic and antibiotic cream

- Passport
- Perfume, lotions, creams
- Phone card
- Photocopied documents (left at home in case yours are lost)
- Postage stamps (if you're traveling in the United States)
- Purse
- Q-tips
- Reading material—books or magazines
- Red Cross knife
- Sewing kit
- Shampoo and toiletries
- Shirts/blouses/tops
- Shoes and sandals
- Silverware, vegetable peeler
- Skirts/slacks
- Sleepwear
- Small mirror
- Soap
- Socks
- Sticky-back notes
- String bag
- Suits/dresses
- Swimsuit
- Tanning lotion and sunscreen
- Tea bags or favorite coffee, small milk pitcher
- TheraFlu
- Toothbrush, toothpaste, floss, toothpicks
- Travel iron

- Traveling clothes

- Turnpike change

- Tweezers, scissors, nail files, nail polish, polish remover

- Umbrella

- Underwear

- Vaseline

- Visine

- Vitamins

- Watch, jewelry

- Water bottle (to fill en route)

- Work materials/notes

► If travel is a regular part of your life, keep prepacked hand luggage at the ready with a few basics: sample-size toiletries; pens, notepaper, blunt scissors, tape, or whatever small office supplies you generally need; underwear, socks, and sleepwear; a small manicure set (if you are flying and aren't checking luggage, omit this). After each trip, refill the bag so that it's ready to go next time.

Is there anything as horrible as starting on a trip? Once you're off, that's all right, but the last moments are earthquake and convulsion, and the feeling that you are a snail being pulled off your rock.

—Anne Morrow Lindbergh
(1930)

► Two or three days before departure, confirm all information: planes, hotels, car rentals, and meetings. It's a little time-consuming, but not nearly as much as running into trouble en route. You can print out your boarding passes 30 hours before departure. Do this. It's quick, and it will save you time at the airport.

► E-mail a copy of your itinerary with a few key phone numbers to several family members or friends so that you can be located quickly in case of an emergency.

▶ Finding your luggage on the carousel among pieces just like it is frustrating. The best two-fer is to get a wildly colored, unique ID tag that flags your attention immediately. Make sure that your name and address aren't readable by passersby, and use your office address and number instead of your home information. You can make your plain black bag stand out by stenciling dog prints or hearts or shamrocks on it with paint. Your luggage is going to get beaten up anyway—you may as well have first crack at it.

▶ If you haven't looked at travel accessories lately, treat yourself. To keep money, passports, boarding passes, credit cards, and licenses safe, money belts go around your waist under your clothes, pouches hang around your neck under your clothes, slim bags strap to your leg under your clothes, and travel scarves hang casually around your neck but are secured to your waistband with straps and contain both large and small pockets that can be worn either next to your body or facing out. The neck pouch is the easiest to get at and is safe as long as it's under your clothes most of the time. But if you don't like that, there's certainly something that will suit you among the many colors, materials, and sizes.

▶ The easiest way to keep track of reimbursable expenses while traveling is to enclose the company expense sheet (or a blank sheet of paper) in a business-size envelope or a large manila envelope, depending on how heavy or light your expenses usually are. Put all receipts in the envelope and record the required details on the expense sheet or paper. When you return, everything is in one place.

▶ Secure-locking baggies have many travel uses. If you're traveling super-economy, you can carry your wet bar of soap from one hostel to another; bottles of pills can be kept in baggies in case of spilling; items that might leak (pen cartridges and perfume) or that are messy (toothpaste) can travel in them.

▶ While you are on the road, use one of the outer compartments of your luggage for all used clothing; this keeps it separate from clean clothing and makes it easy to put everything from that compartment in the wash when you get home.

▶ In principle, a pleasure trip should provide fun in three parts: while planning it, while traveling, and while processing it afterwards. (Ilka Chase said it best, "To me travel is a triple delight: anticipation, performance, and recollection.") If planning is torture for you, leave it to the people who are going with you or to a professional. If you're planning it, the main decision is whether to go with a tour, make all the arrangements yourself, or combine the two (you make all arrangements, but they include a sightseeing boat trip on the Seine, a bus tour of New York City, a London-by-night tour, a three-day side trip in Thailand, a tour of Italian vineyards, a four-day visit to the castles of the Loire, and other places you can't easily access yourself).

▶ Airplane health:

- That refreshing stream of air coming from the air vents is recirculated air, which is probably full of germs. Portable, battery-operated items to purify the air you're breathing function in a variety of ways; check into them if you always come home from a trip with a cold or the flu.

- Even people without a medical predisposition to blood clots can develop them on long flights. To lessen the chances of a clot, wear very loose clothing (nothing should bind you and interfere with circulation from the waist down), drink as much water as you can (alcohol and caffeine contribute to dehydration, so avoid them), walk the aisles when possible, and otherwise stretch your legs, especially the calves, by lifting your legs and pointing your toes up and down, holding each position for a few seconds. You can get into the habit of keeping your leg muscles moving constantly (think of it as a nervous habit), thus keeping your circulation from pooling. Your seatmates may wonder about you, but you can handle that. It's not a good idea to let the seat bottom press against the back of your upper legs for a long flight. If there are no footrests, place your feet on your carry-on or a makeup case to elevate your legs so that there's no pressure on the back of the legs.

- There are many suggestions for avoiding the piercing and almost unbearable ear pain that some people experience. Probably the best is to take a tissue, gently pinch your nostrils together or otherwise close them off, shut your mouth, and blow down through your nose *when you're taking off*. Many people do this when they're descending, but it's too late then. The damage is done on takeoff (when you usually feel nothing), but you pay for it as the plane descends (when you should repeat the maneuver). Babies and small children, who have even smaller ear canals, need to be swallowing something. The time to give a bottle or have children drink something is when you're taking off (and, again, on descent).

▶ Print out details about other flights leaving for your destination the same day as yours. If anything disrupts your flight, you'll know what other flights you can catch. It's almost always more effective to call the airline to rebook than to wait in line and hope that a counter attendant can help you.

▶ Whether you are traveling domestically or abroad, it doesn't hurt to have a prepaid phone card with you. In the United States, you could find yourself in an area without cell phone service. Abroad, it's very costly to call the United States, unless you have one of the ultra-inexpensive phone cards. A card is also going to be much less expensive than using the hotel phone service.

> *Travel is the most private of pleasures. There is no greater bore than the travel bore. We do not in the least want to hear what he has seen in Hong Kong.*
> —VITA SACKVILLE-WEST
> (1926)

▶ When you are returning from a particularly splendid pleasure trip, take some time on the flight or ship home to single out one to three trip highlights. Everyone will ask, "How was your trip?" You know that they aren't really angling for an invitation to see your photos and hear an hour-by-hour travelogue. They also don't want to hear a simple, "Great!" You have to say something. If you are prepared with a couple of pithy stories, you and they will both be happier. (Note that the most interesting stories are of the things that went wrong. There's no use rhapsodizing over the Alps or the canals in Thailand or telling them how the Panama Canal locks work. They want to hear about your lost luggage and how you had to wear your son's "Mad Dog" T-shirt for a week in Paris.)

Organizing Aids

► Highlighters

► Sticky-back notes

► Phone card

► Luggage ID tags

► Money belt

► Maps

Leisure

> People who know how to employ themselves, always find leisure moments, while those who do nothing are forever in a hurry.
> —MARIE-JEANNE ROLAND
> (1792)

The death of leisure has been announced periodically over the centuries. In 1859, George Eliot wrote, "Leisure is gone—gone where the spinning-wheels are gone, and the pack-horses, and the slow wagons, and the peddlers who brought bargains to the door on sunny afternoons." One wonders what she would think of us today.

Leisure may be in the eye of the beholder, or leisure may be what we are required to create for ourselves.

Tips

► Reduce the amount of time you spend in front of the television (see Chapter 6 for a section on managing your viewing habits), and spend those hours doing something you really like to do, something that will leave you feeling better about yourself than when you started. Don't give up television in favor of things you ought to do. You'll just be resentful, and you can hardly call that use of time "leisure." To make your TV-replacement activity as easy as sinking into a comfortable chair, dedicate a space to your hobby, lay out your equipment, and leave the table ready for your next session before you quit.

▶ If your idea of the ideal weekend is doing nothing, planning nothing, and enjoying every minute, the only thing you need to do is fend off people who have other plans for you. (See Chapter 5, "Dealing with People.")

▶ If you're not happy with your leisure time—or, in fact, if you feel that you don't have a minute to yourself from one week to the next—pinpoint the major sources of the theft of your time. Once you see where the trouble is coming from, you can probably deal with it (for help, see Chapter 5).

- Do your family and friends make demands on you? To maintain relationships, you have to give something. You don't, however, have to give everything; you don't owe your soul or your mental health to anyone. Sometimes it's easier to cut someone out of your life than to decide that they can have just this much of your time, but not that much. Drawing lines requires intelligence, insight, and compassion. But you can do it. Set limits. "I can play tennis with you once a month. That's it." "Mom, I can come to dinner once a month. We can call each other in between times."

- Do your bosses expect you to work nights and weekends? This is the most difficult situation. You have to balance the trade-offs— will your extra time pay off big someday (not too far off)? Or do you have a boss who thinks that this is normal and doesn't particularly give you credit for being a go-getter?

> *I strongly urge you to consciously consider what success means to you. Instead of allowing others or society to determine when you win, you determine it.*
>
> —PAT HEIM (1993)

- Does your spouse, partner, or best friend demand more of your time than you feel is right?

- Are you the problem? After a weekend, for example, do you have trouble remembering just what you did or where the time went? You might need to plan ahead, to lock in place some things that you want to do. The idea of planning leisure time seems counterintuitive, but people with a certain temperament need to do just that in order to feel, on Monday morning, that they've had a wonderful weekend.

- Could you be in a stage of life that has no leisure time in it? If you have small children, work at a challenging job, live in a house that needs repairs, and try to be a good daughter or son to your aging parents, you may indeed have no leisure time. Looking for it, longing for it, and being frustrated at your lack of it will get you nowhere. It's less stressful to go with the flow. Do some self-talk—about the rewards of your family, your job, your home, and your parents, and about

> The multibillion-dollar entertainment and leisure industries notwithstanding, Americans have not learned how to use large amounts of leisure in noncompulsive, personally satisfying ways.
> —JANET SALTZMAN CHAFETZ
> (1974)

how limited this period of your life is. Parents with grown children look back in disbelief at how quickly their parenting years went by. So face the fact that you don't have leisure as you would define it, and find small ways to renew yourself daily.

▶ Keep your leisure hours from feeling like same-old same-old by trying something new. It takes a little planning, but the payoffs can be huge.

- Rent an RV and go to a nearby faraway place (so that the gas bills don't cast a pall over your trip).

- Check out colorful activities that are going on nearly in your backyard, from strawberry festivals to rose festivals, rodeos to flower markets, huge flea markets to hometown baseball games.

Sometimes we're too tired or feel that we're too busy to commit to activities like these, yet, paradoxically, we come home from them with more mental energy than we left with.

- Borrow enough camping gear from a friend to spend a weekend in the wild—even if it's only a local parkground.

- Take up a hobby (see the previous discussion).

- Do something for someone else. Volunteer at a shelter or hospital or children's home, or take a single parent's child to a movie or a game. There's nothing that makes you feel more grateful for the time you have than seeing how others spend theirs. If you have a metaphysical bent, you can attribute this to the theory that by giving what you need (time), you receive the same back.

- Plan a small project for your backyard or your home: a solar fountain, a revolving coffee table, an outdoor or indoor storage bench. Choose something that is not urgently needed, so that you can work on it here and there. In a world in which work rewards are often fleeting, if not intangible, completing a project gives a person a sense of having created something solid, useful, and pleasing.

▶ Iris Murdoch says, "One of the secrets of a happy life is continuous small treats." Your leisure time need not be filled with big plans. You will feel just as refreshed after a weekend if you have arranged a few small treats for yourself: a nap in a hammock, a glass of iced tea or a cold

> *To be quite oneself one must first waste a little time.*
> —ELIZABETH BOWEN (1935)

beer with a new book, a picnic in the park, a walk through an unfamiliar part of town, or buying yourself a CD you've been wanting.

▶ And, finally, do enjoy some "wasted" time: daydreaming, napping, doodling, working crossword or sudoku puzzles, chatting with a stranger, playing statues with a child, watching ants, staring out the window, or making a loaf of bread because you can. These small buffers refresh us and give our subconscious minds time to come up with ideas and solutions that may benefit us another time. They are not quantifiable ("I worked X hours and made X dollars"), and you don't have anything to show for them, but they are priceless all the same. They may actually be what we mean by "leisure."

Organizing Aids

▶ Thinking cap

Index

About the Author

Rosalie Maggio is the award-winning author of 22 books, including *The Art of Talking to Anyone* and the two-million-copy bestseller *How to Say It: Words, Phrases, Sentences, and Paragraphs for Every Situation.*